525

THE LIVING WORD COMMENTARY

Editor
Everett Ferguson

Associate Editors
Abraham J. Malherbe · John David Stewart

The Letters of Paul to
The Thessalonians

The Letters of Paul to
The Thessalonians

Raymond C. Kelcy

πᾶσα γραφὴ
θεόπνευστος

R. B. SWEET CO., INC.

Austin, Texas 78751

Printing History
First Printing, September, 1968
Second Printing, September, 1969
Third Printing, February, 1975

LIBRARY OF CONGRESS CARD NUMBER
68–55947

Acknowledgement

This commentary is based on the text of the Revised Standard Version of the Bible, copyrighted 1946 and 1952 by the Division of Christian Education, National Council of Churches, and used by permission.

Writers in *The Living Word Commentary* series have been given freedom to develop their own understanding of the biblical text. As long as a fair statement is given to alternative interpretations, each writer has been permitted to state his own conclusions. Beyond the general editorial policies, the editors have sought no artificial uniformity, and differences are allowed free expression. A writer is responsible for his contribution alone, and the views expressed are not necessarily the views of the editors or publisher.

Contents

I

Introduction to
1 Thessalonians

THE CITY OF THESSALONICA

IN 315 B.C. THE Macedonian king, Cassander, built a new city near the site of the ancient town of Therma. The wife of Cassander was named "Thessalonica." She was a daughter of the king of Macedonia, Philip II, and a step-sister of Alexander the Great. Cassander named the new city in honor of her.

Thessalonica, being on the Egnatian Road and having a natural harbor, grew rapidly in size and wealth. Rome, after conquering the city in 168 B.C., made it the capital of one of the four provinces into which she divided Macedonia. Thessalonica, after the area became one province, was made capital of the whole territory. It continued to advance and became an important commercial center of the Roman Empire. When Paul first arrived there with the gospel, Thessalonica was an important, though wicked, city. It remained essentially Greek in nature though its population consisted of Romans, Greeks, and Jews, giving it somewhat a cosmopolitan nature.

Since the first century Thessalonica has had an interesting history. It was captured by the Saracens in A.D. 904, by the Normans in A.D. 1185, and by the Turks in A.D. 1430. The Turks held it until it was captured by the Greeks in 1912. Today, under the name of "Salonika," it is still a prosperous, important Greek city.

ESTABLISHMENT OF THE CHURCH

On the second missionary tour, in company with Silas, Timothy, and Luke, Paul, in response to the "Macedonian Call," went to Philippi and began a church in that city (Acts 16:6f.). After being asked by the city officials to leave Philippi, Paul, Silas, and perhaps Timothy, travelled another hundred miles and came to Thessalonica (Acts 17:1-9).

In Thessalonica Paul reasoned in the Jewish synagogue over a period of about three weeks. He showed from the Old Testament scriptures that the death and resurrection of Christ were a necessity, maintaining that the Jesus whom he proclaimed had fulfilled these prophecies and was that Christ. However, though Luke does not discuss it in Acts, Paul's ministry in Thessalonica extended to the Gentiles (1 Thess. 1:9ff.). In this ministry his approach would naturally be quite different from that wherein he taught in the synagogue of the Jews. Certain points which received emphasis in his preaching to the Gentiles may be ascertained from a reading of 1 Thessalonians. These will be discussed as they appear in the text.

Paul found Thessalonica to be quite a productive field. His preaching resulted in the conversion of "some" Jews, of "a great many of the devout Greeks," and "not a few of the leading women" (Acts 17:4). There were also a number of converts from among the heathen as certain passages in the epistle indicate (e.g., 1:9; 2:14).

How long did Paul remain in Thessalonica? Some think that he must have remained for a period of several months. They point out that the weeks mentioned in Acts 17:2 were

8

spent in connection with the synagogue; they maintain that, in addition, a considerable time must have been spent among the Gentiles. They point to other facts which, to them, indicate a stay longer than three weeks—facts such as Paul's engaging in manual labor while in Thessalonica (1 Thess. 2:9), and his receiving help from Philippi more than once (Phil. 4:16). They feel that Paul would not likely have resorted to his manual occupation if his stay in Thessalonica had been for only two or three weeks and that, Philippi being a hundred miles away, a period of longer than two or three weeks is indicated by his receiving help from that city more than once. Furthermore, they see in such passages as 1 Thessalonians 2:7, 11 indications of Paul's dealing with certain ones in a personal way—possibly by way of visitation among various homes. All of this does seem to point to a stay which was longer than three weeks.

There are those, however, who think Paul remained in Thessalonica only during the period of the three weeks mentioned in Acts 17:2. They maintain three or four weeks was enough time for Paul to engage in manual labor—that, in fact, a man with such limited means as that of Paul would likely feel the need of earning some money even within so short a period. They suggest that it was possible for messengers from Philippi to come to Paul with assistance even more than once during the short interval. Morris suggests (see bibliography, p. 20) that the Greek construction of Philippians 4:16 does not make it certain that Paul received help from Philippi more than once while he was in Thessalonica; he says that the construction could mean that Paul received help from the Philippians both when he was in Thessalonica and, more than once, when he was in other places. He points to 1 Thessalonians 2:18 as a passage containing the same idiomatic expression indicating a plurality or a number of times. He maintains that the expression "both . . . and" of Philippians 4:16 seems to indicate a reference to two different situations. Some who hold to the idea of a short stay in Thessalonica say that a short ministry is in harmony with the hurried nature of Paul's labors in other cities at about this same time—the nature of an intensified campaign. In addition, they point to Luke's account of Paul's ministry in cities such as Corinth (Acts 18:6), Ephesus (Acts 19:8-10), and Rome (Acts 28:9); they call attention to the fact that in these instances Luke specifically makes mention of his turning his attention to the Gentiles. They suggest that if Paul had turned from a ministry among the Jews in Thessalonica to an intense ministry among the Gentiles then it is likely that Luke would have mentioned it.

The statement of Luke in Acts 17:2 regarding the three weeks during which Paul was teaching in the synagogue does not necessarily limit the entire ministry in Thessalonica to a period of only three weeks. It could very well have been longer. Luke does not always give a detailed chronology. It cannot be determined with certainty just how long the stay in Thessalonica was; however, it could not have been longer than a few months even if the highest estimate is accepted.

The success of Paul and his helpers aroused the envy of the unbelieving Jews, and a strong opposition arose against the missionaries. Jewish opposition was almost regularly encountered by Paul. In Antioch of Pisidia (Acts 13:45, 50), in Lystra (Acts 14:19), in Corinth (Acts 18:12), in Ephesus (Acts 19:9), and in other cities where Paul preached he found determined and vicious opposition. In certain instances Jewish enemies would pursue Paul from one city to another (Acts 14:19; 17:13). Against this background Paul's violent denunciation of the Jewish persecutors can be better understood (1 Thess. 2:14-16).

OCCASION OF 1 THESSALONIANS

After the persecution became intense in Thessalonica, the brethren sent Paul and Silas away to Beroea where they preached in the synagogue (Acts 17:10). The Jews here were "more noble" than were those of Thessalonica; their nobility is seen in the fact that they heard the message with readiness and examined the scriptures in order to test the genuineness of that message (Acts 17:11). As a result a large number believed (vs. 12). However, the arrival of persecuting Jews from Thessalonica caused the brethren to send Paul away; Timothy and Silas remained in Beroea (vss. 13, 14). Upon Paul's arrival in Athens he sent those who had accompanied him back to Beroea with instructions for Silas and Timothy to join him as soon as possible (vs. 15). Paul had very little success in Athens; in fact, he met derision and scorn (vss. 32-34). Having met severe opposition in three successive cities (Acts 16:19-39; 17:5-9; 17:13), and having met with scorn in Athens (Acts 17:32), Paul's spirits must have been quite low when he arrived in the large, wicked city of Corinth. There he lived with Aquila and Priscilla and preached Christ in the synagogue every sabbath (Acts 18:1-4).

Soon after Paul's arrival in Corinth, Silas and Timothy came from Macedonia (Acts 18:5). Timothy conveyed to Paul news about the Thessalonian church (1 Thess. 2:6). In the narrative in Acts Luke does not mention Timothy's accompanying Paul and Silas from Philippi to Thessalonica (16:25-17:4). Luke's use of "they" shows that Luke himself did not accompany them (17:1). It may be that Timothy did and that Luke did not mention the fact since he was discussing the imprisonment of Paul and Silas and their subsequent release and departure. Or, it may be that Timothy did not accompany them and that he came to Thessalonica a short time later. Again, in the Acts narrative, Luke tells of the sending away of Paul and Silas to Beroea, making no mention of Timothy (Acts 17:10). The exact itinerary of Timothy is obscure; however, mention is specifically made of Silas and Timothy being left at Beroea when Paul departed for Athens (Acts 17:14). If Timothy did not accompany them to Beroea, then he had joined them there later. From Paul's statement about being left alone in Athens and sending Timothy to Thessalonica, it is safe to conclude that Timothy had come to Athens in compliance with Paul's request (1 Thess. 3:2). Also, since the word "alone" is in the plural, it seems safe to conclude that Silas, too, had come to Athens and cooperated in the sending of Timothy. Likely Paul later sent Silas to Macedonia, probably to Philippi. It is certain that when both Timothy and Silas rejoined Paul in Corinth they had just come from Macedonia (Acts 18:5; cf. 2 Cor. 11:9).

Paul knew that he had left the infant church in Thessalonica exposed to the malignity of those who had so vehemently opposed him. He was troubled regarding their safety; he doubtless wondered if his short ministry there had grounded them to the extent that they would endure. He longed to see these Christians "face to face" soon after he left them; he more than once desired to visit them but had not been able to carry out this desire (1 Thess. 2:17, 18). Being unable to return, he sent Timothy to strengthen and encourage the Thessalonians.

Thanksgiving and rejoicing are predominant throughout the first three chapters of 1 Thessalonians. The report brought by Timothy did much to relieve Paul's anxieties and caused him to write the epistle from which the substance of Timothy's report can be learned. The Thessalonians had endured persecution with courage and were remaining steadfast; they were eager to see Paul again; they were still devoted to him and held him as a dear friend (3:6-8). All of this was most encouraging to Paul.

Some feel that Paul's defensive tone in chapter 2 indicates that Timothy had brought news of attempts in Thessalonica to defeat the church by vilification of Paul and his helpers. They feel that enemies were disparaging both the work and the character of these ministers: they were charging them with being teachers of falsehood, preaching out of motives of greed, and wielding a bad influence. They think these enemies were saying that Paul had shown his lack of concern by failing to visit the church. This is all possible. It may be that there were such enemies who were spreading such reports in Thessalonica and that Paul is answering them. On the other hand, there is no explicit statement to the effect that there were enemies in Thessalonica who were making such charges. It is not conclusive as in 2 Corinthians and Galatians where Paul is definitely answering charges of enemies. The defense is quite different in tone. It may be that the defense is not so much one of answering specific charges as that of drawing a distinction between Paul and his helpers and the wandering charlatans of that day. The antithetic style used in the contrast would give the readers assurance of the genuineness of the missionaries and of their labors.

There was some disturbance in the church over matters pertaining to the second coming of Christ. There seems to have been anxiety on the part of some regarding their loved ones who had died. Will those who are alive at the time of the second coming have an advantage over the dead (4:13-18)? The time of Christ's coming seems also to have been a matter for speculation (5:1ff.). It may be that something which Paul had previously taught was being perverted.

Of course there was always the problem of the heathen world and the temptations it offered. Paul can remember that the Thessalonians have turned from immoral practices of a heinous nature; he is ever mindful of the danger of their returning to this type of life. Something of this danger was likely also included in the report of Timothy (4:1-8).

The occasion, then, of 1 Thessalonians was the report brought to Paul by Timothy. The purposes Paul had in mind when writing may be said to be fourfold: (1) to express joy and gratitude over the Thessalonians' fidelity to God and their continued loyalty to Paul and his helpers; (2) to set forth a defense of the missionaries and their ministry in Thessalonica; (3) to encourage the Thessalonians to remain faithful in the face of trials; (4) to give instruction and counsel relative to doctrinal and practical matters.

AUTHORSHIP, PLACE OF WRITING, AND DATE

The authenticity and the integrity of 1 Thessalonians are admitted today by practically all New Testament scholars. The internal evidence is all that could be desired; the vocabulary is that of Paul and the epistle is Pauline in both style and thought. Paul associates the names of Silvanus (Silas) and Timothy with his own in the opening verse; they share with Paul the sentiments expressed in the letter. Silvanus had worked with Paul in establishing the church in Thessalonica (Acts 17:4). It is possible that Timothy had also helped. They are both with Paul in Corinth at the time of writing (Acts 18:5; 2 Cor. 1:19; 1 Thess. 1:1). They share with Paul a deep interest in the church in Thessalonica.

External evidence for the authenticity of the epistle is likewise strong. The epistle is found in the Syriac vulgate and in the Old Latin Versions. It was included in Marcion's canon (*circa* A.D. 140) and in the Roman Canon which was preserved in the Muratorian Fragment (*circa* A.D. 170). Irenaeus quotes the epistle by name (*circa* A.D. 180, *Against Heresies* V, 6, 1), and there are frequent references in the Fathers from Irenaeus onward.

Luke reports the arrival of Timothy and Silas in Corinth (Acts 18:5), and in the epistle Paul mentions Timothy's recent arrival (3:6). In the epistle the names of Silvanus, Timothy, and Paul are linked together in greeting the Thessalonians (1:1). The evidence thus points to Corinth as the place from which the epistle was written.

Paul wrote 1 Thessalonians while on the second missionary journey at the time designated in Acts 18:5. The date of Paul's ministry at this time is the most nearly certain date in Pauline chronology; this makes possible the dating of the epistle with a great degree of accuracy, though the year and month have not definitely been settled. The proconsulship of Gallio, mentioned by Luke as being during this time (Acts 18:12), is the incident that makes the dating rather certain. An inscription found at Delphi in 1909 preserves a message from the Emperor Claudius to the citizens of Delphi. Gallio is mentioned along with information which makes possible the dating of his arrival in Corinth during the first half of the year A.D. 52. It is not known at what stage of his proconsulship Paul appeared before him, nor is it known how long Paul had been in Corinth prior to the arrival of Gallio. Another uncertainty comes from the fact that proconsuls sometimes had a tenure of office lasting for two years instead of one. However, even with these uncertainties, no error of consequence can be made if the epistle is dated A.D. 51-52. This is approximate and a variation of several months, either earlier or later, must be allowed.

VALUE OF 1 THESSALONIANS

Paul's first epistle to the Thessalonians has special significance for the following reasons:

(1) It is among the earliest, if not the earliest, of Paul's epistles. There is a great deal of uncertainty about the dating of Galatians and some scholars think it to be first. At any rate, 1 Thessalonians is among the earliest, being written about A.D. 51-52; some scholars date it as early as A.D. 50. It thus reflects the teaching and belief of the church at a very early stage, a time about twenty years after the resurrection of Christ.

(2) A number of the great Pauline doctrines are found in 1 Thessalonians, though some of them receive only slight mention. There is great emphasis on the doctrine of God as contrasted with the false gods whom the Thessalonians formerly worshipped. The writers refer to God as "Father" in a way which shows that the term was in general use (1:1; 3:11; 3:13). They look to God as the source of the gospel, as the one who approved them for their work, as the

INTRODUCTION

one to whose verdict they submit, as the one upon whom they depend as the true author of all that is good (2:2-10; 3:11; 5:23). Likewise, they direct the attention of the Thessalonians to God as the source of their every need (1:4, 8, 9; 2:12; 3:11; 4:5; 5:23f.).

The epistle presents a highly exalted view of Christ. The writers refer to Christ as God's Son (1:10). They unite the name of Christ with that of the Father in such a way as to emphasize the deity of Christ (1:1; 3:11). They designate him as "Lord" (e.g. 1:1; 2:1), a title which was a common one for God among the Jews of the time. They assign to Christ, along with the Father, an important part in the events of the last day (3:13; 4:6, 17; 5:2). They look to Christ, no less than to the Father, as the author of their commission (2:6; 3:2). They enforce their charges "in" or "by" Christ (4:1; 5:27).

There is no elaboration on the doctrine of the Holy Spirit. The writers assert that their gospel had come to the Thessalonians "in the Holy Spirit" (1:5); they assure the Thessalonians that the joy they had shown in the midst of persecution was "inspired by the Holy Spirit" (1:6); they plead with them not to "quench the Spirit" (5:19); they remind them that to fall into sin is to be guilty of disregarding God "who gives his Holy Spirit to you" (4:8).

Regarding the doctrine of salvation, the vicarious death of Christ is mentioned (5:10); Jesus is described as the one "who delivers us from the wrath to come" (1:10). Salvation is implied as a result of union with Christ (1:1), and life with Christ is said to be the purpose of Christ's death (5:10). Eternal life with Christ is designated as the goal of the Christian's hope (4:17).

Of special significance in 1 Thessalonians is the emphasis on the second coming of Christ and the resurrection and matters related to these events. This eschatological emphasis has, in recent years, caused a renewed interest in the Thessalonian letters. Anxieties and speculations in Thessalonica caused the writers to pen two of the most significant

16

eschatological passages in the New Testament: (1) 4:13-18, in which the Thessalonians are given assurance that the living saints will have no advantage over the dead at the time of Christ's coming. The dead will rise before the living are caught up and all shall together go up to meet the Lord; (2) 5:1-11, in which the uncertainty of the time of the Lord's coming is discussed and in which the Thessalonians are urged to live so as to be in a constant state of readiness. The writers look to a future life with Christ (5:10); they refer to the second coming of Christ in sections which appear at the close of each chapter (1:10; 2:19; 3:13; 4:15-17; 5:23).

There is, in 1 Thessalonians, the characteristically Pauline emphasis on the Christian virtues and on moral and ethical conduct. Works are viewed as a natural fruit of faith, labor as a fruit of love, and steadfastness as a fruit of hope (1:3). Sanctification is God's will for man (4:3) and the ultimate goal is the sanctification of the complete person (5:23). Moreover, sanctification involves maintaining certain standards of purity and whoever rejects these standards rejects God (4:3-8). Christians are to love one another, to attend to their own business, to work in order to earn a living, to live in such a way as to secure the respect of those who are not Christians (4:9-12). In view of the uncertainty of the Lord's return and since Christians belong to the day, being children of light, they are to live in watchfulness and sobriety (5:1-8). They are to be at peace among themselves, return good for evil, rejoice, pray, etc. (5:12ff.).

(3) First Thessalonians gives a wonderful insight into the evangelistic message of Paul. Paul gives a recapitulation of some of the things he had preached in Thessalonica, conveying to the reader just what the substance of apostolic preaching was in its early form. Paul had declared the futility of idol worship; he had preached "a living and true God"; he had proclaimed the deity, the death, the resurrection, and the second coming of Jesus (1:9f.). He had made clear to the Thessalonians that the message delivered by

him and his associates was the word of God (2:13). In this connection Paul's appeal to what the Thessalonians already know in confirmation of what he is writing reveals something of instructions he had given them (e.g., 2:10-12; 3:3f.; 4:1f.; 4:9; 5:1f.).

(4) First Thessalonians, more than any other of Paul's letters, reveals the attitude and feelings of the great apostle toward his converts. He thanked God for them and prayed constantly for them (1:2); he had, while among them, dealt gently with them as a nurse taking care of her own children (2:7); he had admonished in a way similar to the way a father admonishes his children (2:11); he had felt such anxiety on their behalf that he was willing to be deprived of Timothy's presence in order that Timothy might go to Thessalonica (3:1f.); he had felt a great renewal of spirit after Timothy's return to him with a favorable report (3:6ff.); he assured the Thessalonians that they were his joy and crown (2:19f.).

OUTLINE

C. Instructions regarding the second coming of Christ, 4:13-18
D. Instructions regarding the time of the second coming, 5:1-11
E. A series of practical exhortations, 5:12-22
F. Concluding matters, 5:23-28

SELECTED BIBLIOGRAPHY

Commentaries on the Greek Text

ELLICOTT, CHARLES JOHN. *A Critical and Grammatical Commentary on St. Paul's Epistles to the Thessalonians.* Grand Rapids: Zondervan Publishing House, 1957 reprint of 1861 edition.

FRAME, JAMES EVERETT. *A Critical and Exegetical Commentary on the Epistles of St. Paul to the Thessalonians.* (International Critical Commentary) Edinburgh: T. & T. Clark, 1953 reprint of 1912 edition.

LIGHTFOOT, J. B. *Notes on the Epistles of St. Paul: I and II Thessalonians, I Corinthians 1-7, Romans 1-7, Ephesians 1:1-14.* Grand Rapids: Zondervan Publishing House, 1957 reprint of 1895 edition.

MILLIGAN, GEORGE. *St Paul's Epistles to the Thessalonians.* Grand Rapids: Wm. B. Eerdmans Publishing Co., 1952 reprint of 1908 edition.

MOFFATT, JAMES. *The First and Second Epistles to the Thessalonians.* (The Expositor's Greek Testament) Grand Rapids: Wm. B. Eerdmans Publishing Company, 1956 reprint.

Commentaries Based on English Translations

BAILEY, JOHN W. "First and Second Thessalonians," *Interpreter's Bible*, Vol. XI. New York: Abingdon, 1955.

BARCLAY, WILLIAM. *The Letters to the Philippians, Colossians, and Thessalonians.* Philadelphia: The Westminster Press, 1959.

INTRODUCTION

HENDRIKSEN, WILLIAM. *Exposition of I and II Thessalonians.* Grand Rapids: Baker Book House, 1955.

LENSKI, R. C. H. *The Interpretation of St. Paul's Epistles to the Colossians, to the Thessalonians, to Timothy, to Titus and to Philemon.* Columbus: The Wartburg Press, 1956.

McGARVEY, J. W. and PHILIP Y. PENDLETON. *Thessalonians, Corinthians, Galatians and Romans.* Cincinnati: The Standard Publishing Co., 1916.

MORRIS, LEON. *The First and Second Epistles to the Thessalonians.* (New International Commentary on the New Testament) Grand Rapids: Wm. B. Eerdmans Publishing Co., 1959.

II

The First Letter
of Paul
to the Thessalonians

SALUTATION, 1:1

[1] THE NAMES of the three who unite to greet the Thessalonians were well known. They were together in Corinth at the time of the writing of the epistle (Acts 18:5). Silvanus was a Roman citizen and this was his Roman name. Luke calls him by his Hebrew name, Silas, and refers to him as a prophet (Acts 15:27, 32). Paul had chosen him for his companion for the second missionary journey (Acts 15:40); he had helped Paul in establishing the church in Thessalonica (Acts 17:1-4). Timothy was another who accompanied Paul on the second missionary journey (Acts 16:1ff.). Luke does not mention Timothy's being with Paul and Silas at the time of the establishing of the church in Thessalonica; there is a possibility that he was there and that Luke did not choose to include it in the Acts narrative (see Introduction). Later, Timothy was the one selected to go to Thessalonica to strengthen and exhort the Christians there (1 Thess. 3:1ff.); he returned to Paul

¹ **Paul, Silvanus, and Timothy, To the church of the Thessalonians in God the Father and the Lord Jesus Christ: Grace to you and peace.**

---

while Paul was in Corinth and brought good news about the church in Thessalonica (1 Thess. 3:6). All three of these men—**Paul, Silvanus, and Timothy**—speak to the church through this epistle; however, the style and the vocabulary are truly Pauline. Paul adds nothing to his name to indicate the character in which he wrote. It is only in the two epistles to the Thessalonians that Paul fails to add something explanatory after his name; it is only in Philemon and in the letters to the Macedonian churches (1, 2 Thessalonians and Philippians) that Paul does not mention his apostleship in the salutation. The three simply refer to themselves by their names, indicating a healthy relation between writers and readers. It is the sort of friendly greeting to be expected as prefatory to earnest teaching and exhortation.

Second in the epistolary address is a description of the recipients of the epistle. They are described as **the church of the Thessalonians** with reference to the city in which they lived. Paul uses the word "church" to designate those who have heard and accepted the call of God to spiritual life and who thus compose a spiritual body. He addresses "the churches of Galatia" (Gal. 1:2), thinking of each church locally in a district. He here uses the word in a local sense as he greets the Thessalonians. When he later affirms that "Christ is the head of the church, his body," he is thinking of God's people in a universal sense (Eph. 5:23). The **church of the Thessalonians** addressed is in the spiritual realm of **God the Father and the Lord Jesus Christ**. The idea of God as Father is an important part of Paul's teaching (cf. Gal. 4:4-7; Rom. 8:12-17).

Something of Paul's Christology is seen in this opening verse. That he considered both **God** and **Christ** as proper names is evidenced by the absence of the definite article from each. He associates the Father and the Son in the closest possible fashion, showing his exalted view of the person of Christ. Further, the combination of the human name **Jesus; Christ,** the Greek form of the Hebrew "Messiah"; and **Lord,** the regular word for Jehovah in the Septuagint, presents the conception of a person who can be considered "God" with all the implications of that divine name. The concept of the "Lord Jesus Christ" is quite a vital one in the New Testament. Quoting the words of David in Psalm 110:1, "The Lord says to my Lord: Sit at my right hand, till I make your enemies your footstool," Peter, in his Pentecost sermon, went ahead to show that David's words have been fulfilled in Jesus of Nazareth. "God has made him both Lord and Christ, this Jesus whom you crucified," declared Peter (Acts 2:34ff.). In the same vein Paul said, "We proclaim Jesus as Lord" (2 Cor. 4:5). This was the main burden of Paul's preaching. Paul also taught the necessity of a corresponding confession on the part of man (Phil. 2:9ff.; Rom. 10:9).

According to the pattern ordinarily found in letters of that day, the names of the writers and of the recipients are followed by a greeting. The greeting is in the words, **Grace to you and peace.** The expression appears to be a combination of the Greek and Hebrew forms of greeting. **Grace** epitomizes all the blessings which God bestows through Christ; **peace** denotes the blessed result which comes to those who receive this grace. This greeting occurs at the beginning of all of Paul's epistles except that in the letters to Timothy and to Titus "mercy" is added.

Thanksgiving and Defense, Chapters 1–3

In this first major section of the epistle, Paul and his companions express gratitude for the Thessalonians, assuring them that they pray for them, that they remember their great Christian qualities, and that they know the Thessalonians have been chosen of God (1:2-4). They proceed to

give reasons for being assured of God's having chosen the
Thessalonians, recalling the power which had accompanied
the preaching and pointing to the afflictions in the midst of
which the Thessalonians had received the gospel (1:5, 6).
Further, they describe the subsequent widespread example
which the Thessalonians have been to others. A further
cause for rejoicing is the fact that the writers' ministry in
Thessalonica and the consequent turning of the Thessalonians from idols to the true God had become common knowledge over a wide area and was being discussed in many
places (1:7-10).

Paul and his helpers proceed to elaborate upon the
character of their ministry in Thessalonica. They had labored in the face of persecution. They deny having had
improper motives; their desire had been to please God and
not man. They have never used flattery nor have they
sought the glory of men. They remind the Thessalonians of
the gentleness with which they had dealt with them and of
their engaging in manual labor so as to avoid being burden-
some to the Thessalonians. They call both God and the
readers to witness as to their holy and righteous conduct;
they remind the readers that, when they had been among
them, they had exhorted them as a father (2:1-12).

The writers next recall the favorable response which the
Thessalonians had given to the message. They thank God
that the Thessalonians had received the message for what it
was, the word of God. They then call attention to the fact
that the Thessalonians, in bearing persecution at the hands
of their countrymen, were imitating the churches of Judea
which had suffered at the hands of unbelieving Jews. They
then proceed to launch a burning attack against the unbelieving Jews (2:13-16).

Next, the writers assure the Thessalonians that they
have sorely missed them and have been with them in heart.
It may be that this is said in reply to enemies who have said
that the missionaries have forgotten the Thessalonians, but
this cannot be certain. It may be that they are giving this

² We give thanks to God always for you all, constantly
mentioning you in our prayers,

---

assurance by way of encouragement. They have wanted to
return—and here Paul emphasizes his own personal desire,
"I Paul,"—but have been hindered by Satan. However, the
Thessalonians are assured that they are the glory and joy of
the writers even at the time they are writing (2:17-20).

Continuing in the vein of defense, the writers assure the
Thessalonian Christians that their concern for them has
been great. In fact, their concern had become so great that
they decided that Timothy should visit Thessalonica to
comfort and strengthen the Christians and that he might
return with news about them. The writers desired that
Timothy help the Thessalonian Christians to the end that
they might not be moved by afflictions. They remind their
readers that they had, when with them, told them that
afflictions would come (3:1-5).

Now, in company with Silvanus, Timothy has returned
to Paul; the three are writing to their beloved friends. Paul
is rejoicing over the news brought by Timothy: the Thessalonians are continuing in the faith and earnestly desire to
see Paul and the others. The writers have been comforted
through the faith of the Thessalonians; in fact, they feel
that life has returned. They assure the readers that they
continue to pray that they might see them and supply any
deficiencies which may exist among them (3:6-10).

Paul and his helpers express a prayer that the Father
and the Son will direct them to the Thessalonians and that
the Lord will help the Thessalonians to increase in love
toward one another and toward others. They pray that God
will establish the Thessalonians so that they may appear
before God "unblamable in holiness" (3:11-13).

Expression of Gratitude for the Thessalonians, 1:2–4

[2] Paul almost invariably has some form of thanksgiving at the beginning of his letters. At the time he writes this

[3] remembering before our God and Father your work of faith and labor of love and steadfastness of hope in our Lord Jesus Christ.

---

letter, the news Timothy has brought about the Thessalonian church so encourages him and revives him that his heart is filled with thanksgiving and he tells the Thessalonians how thankful he is for them. Silvanus and Timothy also share this gratitude with Paul. The use of the present tense, **We give thanks,** and the adverb, **always,** emphasize the constancy of the thanksgiving.

Three participial clauses modify the expression, **We give thanks.** The first of these, **constantly mentioning you in our prayers,** has a temporal significance and tells when the thanksgiving was done. It is when Paul and his companions pray to God that they make mention of the Thessalonians and thank God for them. This assurance given by the writers to the Thessalonians about remembering them in prayer would mean much to these young Christians who were surrounded by heathen vices and who were still feeling the bitter persecution which had begun when the missionaries were with them.

[3] The second of the participial clauses modifying **we give thanks** is introduced by the word **remembering.** This clause functions adverbially and is best construed as causal; it states the immediate ground of the thanksgiving. The writers remember the special manifestations of Christian character which the Thessalonians exhibit and these inspire their gratitude. **Remembering,** a present participle, indicates continuous action. This continuous action is further emphasized by the word **constantly** which, according to the punctuation of modern editions of the Greek text, goes with **remembering.** The RSV has chosen to connect **constantly** with **mentioning.** No damage is done to the teaching by this, and such a construction is possible. It is far more likely, however, that the writers were intending to say that they were **remembering constantly.**

In the constant remembrance of the writers was the great triad of faith, love, and hope. Paul brings the three together in a similar expression at the beginning of his letter to the Colossians (1:3-5). He very logically brings the three together as, writing to the Romans, he says: "Therefore, since we are justified by faith, we have peace . . . we rejoice in our hope . . . and hope does not disappoint us because God's love has been poured into our hearts . . ." (Rom. 5:1-5). The best known occurrence of this famous Pauline triad is in the thirteenth chapter of 1 Corinthians: "So faith, hope, and love abide, these three . . ." (vs. 13). Paul attached a great importance to each of the three and he regarded the three as interrelated. One reason for his seeing such importance in these graces may be determined from the passage under consideration; he thanks God for these graces because of what they produce in the lives of those who possess them. Regarding the Thessalonians, he remembers that their **faith** works, their **love** toils, and their **hope** produces **steadfastness.** Faith, if it is living and active, does something (see Heb. 11); when it fails to act, it is dead (James 2:26). Moreover, true love will **labor;** it will spend and be spent in the service of others. The word Paul uses for **labor** indicates strenuous toil. The love of the Thessalonians was more than a verbal declaration; they so loved others that they toiled in their behalf. The third quality remembered unceasingly by the writers was the **steadfastness** of the Thessalonians—their active and heroic constancy in the face of trials. What produced this determined faithfulness? It was their hope. In their hearts there was a certainty that they would share in the future glory of heaven. Hope makes possible the bearing of burdens and the enduring of adversities (cf. Rom. 8:25; 15:4).

The prepositional phrase, **in our Lord Jesus Christ,** is to be connected with the word **hope.** Paul in this way defines the hope which the Thessalonians had. "Of Christ" is a more exact translation than "in Christ"; and since the sec-

⁴ For we know, brethren beloved of God, that he has chosen you;

ond coming of Christ and related events are prominent throughout the epistle, it is safe to consider this as referring to the hope of the Lord's coming. It is in keeping with Greek grammar to consider **of the Lord** as an objective genitive, the Lord himself being the object of hope.

Another phrase, **before our God and Father,** emphasizes the divine presence in which the hope of the Lord is realized. To connect the phrase with **remembering,** as the RSV does, is quite unnatural since it is so far removed from the word in the Greek text. It is much better to connect it with **hope.** That an eschatological sense is intended is borne out by expressions in other parts of the epistle such as "before our Lord Jesus" (2:19) and "before our God and Father" (3:13).

[4] The third of the participial clauses modifying **we give thanks** is rendered: **We know, brethren beloved by God, that he has chosen you.** The affectionate address, **brethren,** is employed quite often in the two letters to the Thessalonians—fourteen times in the first epistle and seven times in the second. As before noted, the first participial clause is temporal, telling when the writers thank God; the second is causal, indicating the immediate ground of the thanksgiving; this third is also causal and designates the ultimate ground of the thanksgiving. In the final analysis the thanksgiving of Paul and his helpers is caused by their knowing that the Thessalonians have been **chosen** or elected by God. To a church composed largely of Gentiles, this would carry great assurance. In former times Israel had been God's chosen people; now God's chosen ones may be those of any race who hear God's call through the gospel and respond to it (see 2 Thess. 2:13, 14; cf. 1 Peter 2:9, 10). Election is conditional upon man's willingness to be chosen and upon his compliance with God's method of choosing. However, even though being chosen is conditional upon

⁵ for our gospel came to you not only in word, but also in
power and in the Holy Spirit and with full conviction. You
know what kind of men we proved to be among you for
your sake.

---

the part of man, it always emanates from the great love of
God. The word **know** gives the confident assurance of the
writers that the readers are objects of God's gracious choosing. They are certain that the conversion of the Thessalonians was genuine. These brethren have been loved by God
and they have been called and chosen by him. The writers
proceed, in the following verses, to set forth their reasons
for being certain that the Thessalonians have been genuinely converted and added to the Lord's church.

Reason for Certainty of Election, 1:5, 6

[5] Having claimed knowledge of the election or the
choosing of the Thessalonians to membership in the family
of God, the writers go ahead to give their reasons for
feeling this certainty. First, they can speak with certainty of
God's having chosen the Thessalonians because of that
which came within their own experience. They speak of **our
gospel**; Paul referred to "my gospel" (Rom. 16:25). Of
course, Paul's gospel was the same gospel preached by
other faithful preachers (see 1 Cor. 15:1-11; cf. Gal. 1:6-9,
11, 12). When Paul and his co-laborers had preached that
gospel in Thessalonica **the Holy Spirit** had unquestionably
been at work through them (see Acts 17:1-9). Paul knows
that the **power** of God was behind their preaching, that it
was not just a matter of speaking words (cf. 1 Cor. 2:1-13;
4:20). They had spoken by inspiration and it was not a
device of human wisdom. There is also the possibility that
Paul may have in mind other miraculous works (cf. Rom.
15:16; 1 Cor. 2:4; 2 Cor. 12:12; Heb. 2:4). Knowing that the
power of God was in the message (cf. 1 Cor. 1:18) and that
the Holy Spirit was the person behind this power, an assurance filled the hearts of the evangelists. This seems to be

the meaning of the phrase, **with full conviction.** It refers to
the conviction or the persuasion that filled the hearts of the
preachers. They knew that God was at work through them,
choosing a people for his own possession.

Having discussed the way in which the gospel had come
to the Thessalonians, the writers proceed, in a comparative
clause, to appeal to the recipients of the letter to bear
witness to the truthfulness of what has just been said. The
comparative clause is introduced by the Greek *kathōs*
which may be translated by such expressions as "just as" or
"as." The RSV failed to capture the full force of the statement by omitting any translation of *kathōs*. The word definitely connects what follows it with what precedes it. In
effect, the writers are saying, "The gospel came to you in
the above manner just as you know what kind of men we
were while we were there." There is an intensely personal
tone in the statement; in reality, the theme of self-defense,
which will be elaborated upon more fully in 2:1-12, is here
begun.

You know appeals to the actual knowledge of the Thessalonians, knowledge of events that had transpired only a
few months prior to the writing of this epistle. This type of
appeal is apparent throughout the Thessalonian letters
(e.g., 2:1, 2; 3:3, 4; 4:2). The Thessalonians can easily
remember these events which the writers call to their remembrance. They know the truthfulness of what Paul is
here saying—that ample evidence had been given that the
speakers were in possession of the Holy Spirit. When Paul
wrote to the Corinthians he reminded them that "the signs
of a true apostle were performed" among them "with signs
and wonders and mighty works" (2 Cor. 12:12). Concerning his ministry in general, Paul spoke of Christ having
worked through him "by the power of signs and wonders,
by the power of the Holy Spirit" (Rom. 15:19). The Thessalonians likewise had seen the power of God at work
through these men. Could it be doubted that God was
working through them? The Thessalonians could also re-

⁶ And you became imitators of us and of the Lord, for you received the word in much affliction, with joy inspired by the Holy Spirit;

---

member the full conviction and assurance manifested by Paul and his helpers. They had not preached with doubts and misgivings but with boldness of belief. Of this Paul now reminds his readers, and he reminds them that it was **for your sake.** The preachers had not worked to promote selfish interests; they had allowed themselves to be used as instruments of God for the sake of those among whom they ministered. Paul is appealing to the power which attended the work of the preachers and to their conviction that they were speaking the very word of God as one of the reasons for his certainty of the genuine conversion and divine choosing of the Thessalonians.

However, the power attending the preachers was not the only evidence they had. They now proceed to discuss the evidence afforded by the effects of their ministry on the lives of the Thessalonians. The conduct of these people was such that it gave to Paul and his helpers real assurance of the genuineness of their conversion.

[6] Paul says, **You became imitators of us and of the Lord.** Later in the epistle Paul speaks of the Thessalonians having become imitators of the Judean churches in suffering at the hands of their own countrymen (2:14). In other passages Paul appeals to Christians to be imitators of him (1 Cor. 4:16; 11:1; Phil. 3:17; 2 Thess. 3:7, 9). He appealed to the members of the church at Ephesus to be "imitators of God" (Eph. 5:21). It should be observed that Paul does not desire any imitation of himself except to the extent that he followed Christ (1 Cor. 11:1). In the present passage he adds **and of the Lord,** showing that he was confident of the fact that he and his companions had imitated the Lord. This shows that the writers were conscious of their own integrity; they know they had lived exemplary lives in the sight of the Thessalonians. That the Thessalonians had

31

been imitators of these faithful men and of the Lord is more evidence of their genuine conversion and of their having been chosen by God.

You received the word tells when the Thessalonians became imitators of the missionaries. The word translated "received" might well be translated "embraced" or "welcomed." Further, the prepositional phrases, **in much affliction,** and, **with joy inspired by the Holy Spirit,** define more clearly what was principally in the minds of the writers when they refer to the imitation of the Thessalonians. **Affliction** is a word indicating difficult trial. Persecution from unbelieving Jews was felt while the missionaries were in Thessalonica. It evidently continued after their departure and, in addition, there was opposition from the pagans (2:14). It was among difficulties that these people had embraced the gospel; they had welcomed it in the midst of adverse conditions.

The much affliction of the Thessalonians was, however, **with joy inspired by the Holy Spirit.** In their hearts there was a gladness which rose above the adversities. In uniting joy with suffering they were most assuredly imitating both Paul and Jesus, both of whom illustrate in an amazing way the possibility of such a combination. However, joy as an accompaniment of pain is not natural. It must come from above. It must have its origin in **the Holy Spirit.** This accounts for the ability of Paul and Silas to sing while imprisoned at Philippi (Acts 16:25), and for the ability of the apostles to rejoice "that they were counted worthy to suffer dishonor for the name" (Acts 5:41). In another passage Paul speaks of rejoicing in sufferings and declares that "suffering produces endurance, and endurance produces character, and character produces hope, and hope does not disappoint us, because God's love has been poured into our hearts through the Holy Spirit which has been given to us" (Rom. 5:1-5). This helps to explain why these Thessalonian Christians could rejoice even while suffering. The imitation, then, of which the writers spoke in the first part of the verse

[7] so that you became an example to all the believers in Macedonia and in Achaia. [8] For not only has the word of the Lord sounded forth from you in Macedonia and Achaia, but your faith in God has gone forth everywhere, so that we need not say anything.

---

consisted of this—that the Thessalonians received the word in much affliction and with joy which had the Holy Spirit as its source.

Example to Others, 1:7–10

[7] As a result of having become imitators of the writers and of the Lord, the Thessalonians have become **an example to all the believers in Macedonia and in Achaia.** These two provinces made up the whole of Greece. Note the order: first an imitator, then **an example.** The extent of one's imitation of the Lord determines the extent to which that one can be an example for the Lord. That the Thessalonian Christians have thus become models for such wide circles of believers may be surprising news to the Thessalonians; it shows, however, the wide extent to which their influence has reached even at the time Paul is writing this letter. They are examples for Christ to others. How great the compliment!

[8] The writers now wish to show that their statement about the extent of the Thessalonians' example is none too strong. From the Thessalonians they declare, **the word has sounded forth in Macedonia and Achaia** and even in a much wider area. The Greek word *exēcheō,* from which "has sounded forth" comes, denotes a sound such as comes from a trumpet or from thunder. There is the idea of reverberation as an echo. The writers are not necessarily saying that the members of the Thessalonian church had evangelized all of this area; they seem rather to be saying that Thessalonica, a city strategically located on the Egnatian Road as well as on a harbor, had become a sounding board from which reports went in all directions. This would

⁹ **For they themselves report concerning us what a welcome we had among you, and how you turned to God from idols, to serve a living and true God,**

---

not have been true of smaller cities in less advantageous positions. Financial aid sent elsewhere was one means whereby this was accomplished (2 Cor. 11:9). Some of the Thessalonians may have travelled and helped spread the report; others who were not Christians may have told what had happened; still others passing through Thessalonica on their way to other places may have had a part. The word **everywhere** surely indicates a wide area; however, it is likely that Paul is employing an expression which somewhat has the nature of rhetorical hyperbole. The writers say **has sounded forth**, using the perfect tense which, in the Greek, indicates that the sound had gone forth and was continuing to go forth even at the time of the writing of the letter.

But in addition to the fact that the word has sounded forth from Thessalonica, the Thessalonians' **faith in God has gone forth everywhere.** Again the writers use the perfect tense showing that their faith had gone forth and continues to do so. What was happening was that others were going to various places and carrying reports about the faith of these Christians. Some of this may have been done by Jews through the synagogues. In fact, when Paul and his helpers went to other places they found reports about the Thessalonians already preceding them so that they **need not say anything.** This must have brought great joy to Paul and his helpers.

[9] The writers are now ready to relate to the Thessalonians the substance of the report which they hear far and wide. They still desire to show that their statement about the widespread influence of the Thessalonians is not too strong. **They report concerning us,** say the writers. They use the present tense which could well be translated, "they keep reporting." It was not a matter which others had

mentioned once in a casual way and then dropped but something which they kept on repeating.

First, the report being heard from others concerns the reception the evangelists had had among the Thessalonians. It was a report concerning the enthusiastic **welcome** they had received. What the writers here say will not only be an encouragement to the Thessalonians by way of praising them for their widespread reputation; it will also serve as a reminder concerning the conduct and methods of the evangelists, letting the Thessalonians know that this was common knowledge in other places. It thus might be considered as being a reply to certain charges which some think were being circulated against these evangelists in their absence.

Second, the report which the evangelists were hearing from others was **how you turned to God from idols.** The Greek word used here is *epistrephō*. Paul uses the word elsewhere regarding the Jews turning to the Lord (2 Cor. 3:16); he also uses the word concerning Christians turning from the gospel and reverting to their former way of life (Gal. 4:9). Jesus used the term when he said, "Unless you turn . . . you will never enter the kingdom of heaven" (Matt. 18:3). The term is employed in Acts 9:35; 11:21; and in passages which are similar to the Thessalonian passage in that they speak of Gentile conversion from idols to the true and living God (Acts 14:15; 15:19; 26:18). **To God** emphasizes the positive side of the turning; **from idols,** the negative side. Separation from idols and dedication to God describe the effect of the gospel on these people. There is a strong contrast in the passage between the idols from which they turned and the God to whom they turned. Nothing is more illustrative of the power of the gospel than the fact that it could cause such turning among people who had been worshipers of idols and whose ancestors had been worshipers of idols. Such a turning involved a rending asunder of strong ties and a repudiation of much that had been held dear. In 1 Corinthians 8:4-13 and 10:14-30 Paul

35

¹⁰ and to wait for his Son from heaven, whom he raised from the dead, Jesus who delivers us from the wrath to come.

---

discusses in greater detail some of the problems faced by those who had turned from idolatry to God.

Why the Thessalonians had turned to God is also being included in the report which the missionaries are hearing in so many places. Paul employs two infinitives in purpose clauses to describe the purpose of the turning. First, it was **to serve a living and true God.** Jehovah as the "living" God has a strong emphasis in the Old Testament (e.g., Deut. 5:26; Josh. 3:10; 1 Sam. 17:26; 2 Kings 19:4, 16). This emphasis, placed in contrast with the lifeless gods of the heathen, is continued in the New Testament (2 Cor. 6:16). Further, the Lord is described as "true" in contrast with the imagined and false gods of paganism (cf. 1 Cor. 8:4-6). The word **serve** means to be a slave. These people had turned to God to become his slaves (cf. Rom. 6:15-23; 12:11; 14:18; 16:18; Eph. 6:7; Col. 3:24). The Greek word used to designate the exclusive service as slaves was not used in a religious sense in pagan writings. Greeks did not consider service to their gods as exclusive and so employed other words to describe such service. In the present passage **to serve** is a present infinitive, denoting linear action and showing that the purpose was to serve God constantly; it was not that of a momentary whim. The Thessalonians had renounced allegiance to their previous ties in order to become slaves of the true God.

[10] The second infinitive showing the purpose of the turning is **to wait.** The waiting is **for his Son from heaven.** The Thessalonians had turned to the true God so that they might lift their faces upward with faith and hope to a returning Lord. Jesus had promised his disciples that he would come again and receive them (John 14:3). While Jesus was ascending, the men in white assured the disciples that Jesus would come again (Acts 1:11). The second

coming of Christ occupies a prominent place in the New Testament; it is an event mentioned here near the end of chapter 1 and is mentioned near the end of each chapter of this epistle (see also Phil. 3:20).

The Son of God for whom the Thessalonians wait is described more fully by the relative clause, **whom he raised from the dead.** Paul here asserts the historical fact of the resurrection of Christ. This historical event was at the center of the preaching described in the New Testament. In sermons to Jewish listeners the resurrection is stressed in order to show that Jesus is the Messiah in fulfilment of prophecy (Acts 2:24-32; 3:15; 4:10; 13:30). The resurrection is also seen to be an integral part of the preaching to the Gentiles (Acts 17:31). Paul's statement in the passage under consideration shows that it had been an important part of the message delivered in Thessalonica. The principal motive in proclaiming the resurrection to Gentiles seems to have been to demonstrate the power of God which has given to the raised and glorified Savior the position he now holds (cf. Eph. 1:15ff.).

The Son of God is further described as **Jesus who delivers us from the wrath to come.** The present participle with the definite article is used and could be translated "the deliverer." The emphasis here is on that from which Jesus saves or delivers—**wrath.** The wrath of God finds emphasis in the New Testament as early as the ministry of John the Baptist (Matt. 3:7). The work which Jesus has done in behalf of man and the work he is now doing is in order to deliver man from the coming wrath of God and to prepare him for eternal fellowship with God. The wrath of which the writers speak in the present passage is that wrath of God which shall be revealed at the time of the second coming of Christ; it is the judgment with which God shall visit the unbelieving world at the end of this age (Acts 17:31; Rom. 2:5; 5:9; Rev. 19:15). Man is unable to grasp fully the significance of the wrath of God. It includes God's activity against all that is evil. It is not to be thought of as

¹ For you yourselves know, brethren, that our visit to you
was not in vain;

---

vindictive passion nor as uncontrollable anger. In fact,
God's wrath must be without the imperfections which char-
acterize any human trait which might be considered analo-
gous. The idea of God's strong feeling against sin and that
part of his nature which calls for retribution must be maintained, even though the finite mind cannot fully grasp it.
The idea of this wrath is brought up by Paul again in this
same letter (cf. 5:2, 3, 9; see also 2 Thess. 1:5-9).

Nature of Paul's Ministry in Thessalonica, 2:1-12

Having expressed thanksgiving for the Thessalonians
based upon knowledge of their having been chosen of God
and having given the reasons for this certainty, Paul now
proceeds to elaborate more fully upon the nature of his
mission in Thessalonica. He had reminded the Thessalonians in 1:5 how the gospel had come to them and the type of
men the missionaries had been in their midst. The first
twelve verses of chapter 2 expand that thought, repeating
the facts contained in that verse and expanding them. However, the tone of this section is obviously different—the
tone of defense. It may be that Paul had learned of opponents in Thessalonica who were misrepresenting him and
his companions. However, there is no explicit statement in
the epistle to the effect that this was happening. It is not so
evident that Paul has opponents whom he is answering. In
2 Corinthians and in Galatians it is quite evident that he is
answering definite charges. Such is possible here but there
is not the same certainty. It may be that the section is no
more than a defense of the missionaries with the view in
mind of drawing a distinction between themselves and the
wandering charlatans of the time.

[1] Addressing the Thessalonians with the affectionate
brethren, Paul appeals to the knowledge of these people
concerning the visit of himself and his companions. He

²but though we had already suffered and been shamefully treated at Philippi, as you know, we had courage in our God to declare to you the gospel of God in the face of great opposition.

---

makes it emphatic: **you yourselves know.** That which others were reporting (1:9), the Thessalonians know from actual experience. There may be in this statement an intention to distinguish what the Thessalonians know to be factual from false reports being made by others; however, as noted above, there is no certainty regarding this. But the fact which the Thessalonians know is this: the visit of Paul and his associates had not been **in vain.** Some (e.g., Moffatt) think the phrase, **not in vain,** means that the work of the preachers was not fruitless; others (e.g., Milligan) think Paul refers to the character or content of the message and not to the results of it. However, it is the visit which Paul says was **not in vain.** The primary meaning of the word translated "vain" is "empty." Paul is thus affirming the earnestness and the purposefulness of their visit. Their "entrance" (ASV) or visit was not a hollow or empty excursion. The purpose of Paul and his companions, when they brought the gospel to Thessalonica, had been genuine. To understand **not in vain** to refer to the purposeful nature of the visit also has the merit of fitting the antithesis described in the statements following.

[2] Verse 2 proceeds to state the opposite of "in vain" and to describe more fully the visit to which reference was made in verse 1. Rather than making a purposeless visit, the missionaries had shown their sincerity and earnestness by boldly preaching the gospel even **in the face of great opposition.** The Thessalonians can well remember these trying circumstances (Acts 17:5-9). Preaching under intense persecution is surely proof of the sincerity of the preachers. And this proof is augmented by the fact that these preachers had only recently come from Philippi where they had been treated with indignity and insult (Acts 16:22-24).

³ For our appeal does not spring from error or uncleanness, nor is it made with guile;

One would not expect a charlatan or a faker to preach with boldness a message in Thessalonica that had already caused great suffering when preached in Philippi. Paul is desirous of showing that their visit had not been in vain; stronger proof could not be found than he here offers. The word which is translated **opposition** is found in some passages where it obviously has reference to inner struggle or effort (e.g., 1 Tim. 6:12; 2 Tim. 4:7; Col. 2:1). Some understand this to be the meaning here. However, the word is sometimes used to refer to external conflict (as Phil. 1:30) and others think that to be the meaning here. The context seems to suggest inner conflict which had risen due to external opposition. It should be noted that the **courage** which Paul claims is said to be **in our God.** This is his way of glorifying God as the source and sphere of their courage. Paul is ever careful to avoid giving credit to self.

[3] With the explanatory **for,** Paul proceeds to elaborate upon the spirit of his ministry in Thessalonica. He wishes to establish further the sincerity and the purity of motive of the preachers. He makes three emphatic denials regarding their preaching or their appeal. First, their appeal did **not spring from error;** it did not have error for its source. The use of the word **error** in this connection (also in 2 Thess. 2:11 and Rom. 1:27) seems to convey the idea of wrongdoing which has moral quality. It does not have reference to honest error but rather to wrong-mindedness. So, the preachers spoke what they knew to be truth and had no intention whatever of deceiving others. Second, their appeal did not spring from **uncleanness,** that is, it did not spring from unclean, impure motives. The word which is translated **uncleanness** is often associated with sexual impurity (e.g., 4:7; Rom. 1:24; Gal. 5:19; Col. 3:5). Many of the ancient religions were associated with moral impurity, and this charge became a rather common one against

⁴ but just as we have been approved by God to be entrusted with the gospel, so we speak, not to please men, but to please God who tests our hearts.

Christians. Possibly some in Thessalonica had accused Paul and his helpers of having carnal, immoral interests. Or it may be that Paul is strongly disavowing such motives in order to describe their ideal ministry in such way as to show the contrast with wandering charlatans who did have such motives. Third, the appeal was not **made with guile.** Whereas the first two denials have reference to the origin of the message, this third denial has reference to the general atmosphere in which the appeal was made. Wandering religious quacks made use of various devices of trickery in order to get a following. Paul's appeal, he declares, was not made in such an atmosphere of cunning or trickery.

[4] The principal statement of verse 4 is **so we speak;** all other statements in the verse in some way relate to this affirmation. Each statement finds its counterpart in the negatives of the preceding verse. First, they had spoken **just as we have been approved by God to be entrusted with the gospel.** The perfect tense, **we have been approved,** indicates not only a past act but also a continuous state. They had been approved and still are approved. The word which Paul uses indicates approval which comes as a result of testing. The word is translated "test" in 5:21 and "examine" in Luke 14:19. God delivered the task of proclaiming the original and pure gospel to men who had proved themselves by undergoing testing. Paul was ever conscious of the divine commission under which he labored (Gal. 1:11, 12; Acts 20:24; Rom. 1:1, 5; Gal. 2:7). In the present passage he is careful to point out that the approval which he and his fellow preachers enjoy is **by God.** This being true, the appeal made by them could not have been from "uncleanness."

Further, Paul and his helpers could not have made their appeal to the people of Thessalonica "with guile" for it was

⁵ For we never used either words of flattery, as you know, or a cloak for greed, as God is witness;

---

their constant desire to speak in such a manner as to please God, **not to please men** (see also Gal. 1:10). Allegiance to God had ever been their primary concern. Paul describes God whom they seek to please as one who tests our hearts (cf. Jer. 11:20; 17:10). He is conscious of the fact that he is discussing motives; in sincere fervor he pleads his case. He is perfectly willing for his soul to be laid bare before the all-seeing eye of God (cf. 1 Cor. 4:5).

[5] The **for** of verse 5 resumes the "for" of verse 3 and introduces a further description of the ministry and the motives of Paul and his helpers while they were in Thessalonica. Paul denies that they had spoken **words of flattery**, a common device of the insincere teacher who is seeking selfish promotion. Paul and his fellow workers had spoken plainly and honestly; they had not attempted to gain the confidence of the Thessalonians by insincere adulation. The Thessalonians know this and Paul calls upon them as witnesses: **as you know.** Insincere words of praise which are designed to promote self are to be avoided by the faithful teacher of the gospel.

Another thing strongly denied by Paul is that they had used **a cloak for greed.** They had not used any kind of pretext (cloak) to cover up the real motive (greed). The word translated **greed** in this passage is translated "covetousness" in some passages (e.g., Rom. 1:29; Eph. 5:3; Col. 3:5). The idea of preaching the gospel with the thought of material gain was especially abhorrent to Paul (see Acts 20:33). He here strongly avows that they had not preached the gospel pretending to love the souls of men, but all the while having covetous designs in their hearts. They had not pursued the work they were doing in an effort to satisfy selfish interests nor with an inner greed for material gain. This is a matter in which self-deception is easy. Others do not know the hidden motives of the heart, but God knows.

⁶ nor did we seek glory from men, whether from you or from others, though we might have made demands as apostles of Christ.

It is interesting to note in this connection that Paul appeals to the Thessalonians to witness the truthfulness of what he says about avoiding the use of flattery, but he appeals to God as witness of the truthfulness of his denial of greed as a motive. Only God can testify regarding a man's motives.

[6] Paul's third denial of this sentence is that he and his companions had sought glory from men. In this they were imitators of their Master (see John 5:41, 44). This adds something to what was said in verse 4. There Paul said that they had not spoken for the purpose of pleasing men. Here his claim is that they had not sought glory or praise from men. They had not come to Thessalonica and worked among the people in a manner that was designed to elicit their praise, nor had they sought such glory anywhere else. Paul here disclaims their desire for popularity. He is not saying that they had not received honor from men nor that they had no right to receive such honor, but merely that they had not sought it.

Over against the fact that they had not sought glory from the Thessalonians is Paul's statement, **though we might have made demands as apostles of Christ.** The Greek word *baros* used here by Paul may be understood in the sense of "weight" or "burden" with reference to their right of maintenance. A form of this word is used in this sense in verse 9 and in 2 Thessalonians 3:8. Or the word could be understood in the derived sense of "authority" or "dignity." This latter seems to be the predominant thought. Paul seems to be saying that they might have insisted on authority in a manner that was somewhat harsh and demanding, in contrast to the gentleness (vs. 7) actually employed.

It is to be observed that Paul here places Timothy and Silvanus in the category of **apostles.** In what sense does he use the term? These men were surely not apostles in the

⁷ But we were gentle * among you, like a nurse taking care of her children. ⁸ So, being affectionately desirous of you, we were ready to share with you not only the gospel of God but also our own selves, because you had become very dear to us.

* Other ancient authorities read *babes*

same sense as were Paul and the twelve (Acts 1:22; Gal. 2:8). One sent with authority is the basic idea in the word "apostle." Paul here uses the word in the sense of missionaries who were sent by the church on a certain mission. Other passages in which the word has a wider signification than the twelve are Galatians 1:19, Acts 14:14, and 2 Corinthians 8:23. In the passage in 2 Corinthians the word is translated "messengers" but the Greek has the word for "apostles."

[7] Paul now turns to discuss the positive side of himself and his helpers. In contrast with the fact that they had not, as apostles, made demands of the Thessalonians was their actual treatment of them. They had not made such demands but had dealt gently with them (cf. 2 Tim. 2:24 where the Greek word is translated "kindly" instead of "gentle"). Rather than making unkindly demands upon the Thessalonians, these unselfish workers had bestowed such tender and loving care upon them as could come only from dedicated hearts filled with love for those to whom they ministered. Paul uses the illustration of a **nurse** handling **her children** to emphasize the affectionate and efficient care which he and his friends had lavished upon the Thessalonians.

[8] The causal participial clause, **being affectionately desirous of you,** gives emphasis to the depth of affection. The verb found here is not used elsewhere in the New Testament. It is a word expressing very strong emotion and a depth of desire. The present tense indicates that the feeling was continuous. The writers, all of the time they were in Thessalonica, longed after the people there with depth of affection. The imperfect, **we were ready,** gives emphasis to

⁹ For you remember our labor and toil, brethren; we
worked night and day, that we might not burden any of
you, while we preached to you the gospel of God.

---

the fact that this magnanimous feeling on the part of the
missionaries was not a momentary impulse but a continued
state. The phrase **our own selves** (Greek, *psuchas*) refers to
the strength, the energy, and the labors of the evangelists as
they spent themselves in service for others. The fact that
they were really placing their own lives in jeopardy in
order to preach to these people was well known to the
Thessalonians.

As Paul began this verse with a tender expression of
affection, so he ends it: **because you had become very dear
to us.** To these preachers souls were more than statistics.
They gave themselves because of their great love for the
people. The adjective *agapētoi* is very closely akin to the
noun *agapē;* it means **very dear** and refers to the specifically Christian quality of love. It is a love that is of a
self-giving character and nowhere in the New Testament is
that fact more forcibly demonstrated than in the attitude of
Paul and his helpers toward the church in Thessalonica.
Here is a picture of preachers who delivered the message
and their hearts along with it. They did not stand aloof from
the people and objectively hand the word to them. They
gave themselves along with their sermons; their preaching
was afire with an obvious care for their hearers. Jesus paid
a great compliment to John the Baptist when he said that
he was "a shining and a burning lamp" (John 5:35). He
spent himself while showing the way to others. And the one
whom Paul imitated "began to teach them many things"
having seen them and having "had compassion on them"
(Mark 6:34).

[9] With **for** in verse 9 Paul further illustrates the fact
that they had not sought glory from men (cf. vs. 6); he also
resumes the idea of gentleness (cf. vs. 7); and he proceeds
to confirm his declaration of verse 8 relative to their will-

45

[10] You are witnesses, and God also, how holy and righteous and blameless was our behavior to you believers;

---

ingness to give themselves. Paul, Silvanus, and Timothy had worked night and day so that they might not be a burden to the Thessalonians. Paul can say you remember, for the labors of the missionaries were well known to the Thessalonians. Wearisome toil is described by the word labor (Greek, *kopos*). It has reference to hard, wearisome, labor which brings on fatigue. Paul includes the word in his list of hardships and sufferings (2 Cor. 6:5; 11:23). The other word used by Paul is the word toil which describes something of the hardship and struggle that accompanied the labor. These two words in combination show that the work done by Paul and his helpers was laborious and wearisome. The self-denying labors of the evangelists are further described by Paul's statement, we worked night and day. Night and day are genitives of time, used here adverbially, indicating that the work was within the night and within the day—not that it was throughout the night and day (as the accusative would indicate). See also Acts 20:34 and 1 Corinthians 4:12.

There were times when Paul received gifts from churches (cf. 2 Cor. 11:8). He received assistance from the Philippians even while he was in Thessalonica (Phil. 4:16). But he refused to receive support from those among whom he labored if such would impose a burden upon them or if it would invite unnecessary criticism from enemies and so hinder the spread of the gospel. It was a case of having a right that he did not exercise and of recognizing that some things which are lawful are not always expedient (cf. 1 Cor. 6:12). Paul's reference to such refusal is a strong argument for his claim that their visit was not in vain.

[10] Continuing to show that the work of the evangelists in Thessalonica had been genuine, Paul now refers to their purity of life. Concerning their manner of life Paul affirms that both the Thessalonians and God are witnesses

¹¹ for you know how, like a father with his children, we
exhorted each one of you and encouraged you and charged
you

---

to the truthfulness of what he here says. **Holy** is a term
describing dedication to the service of God; **righteous** indicates conformity to God's norm for living; **blameless** emphasizes in a negative way the absence of reproach. **You
believers** designates Christians. Paul's mention of their conduct among the believers does not imply that they had
acted differently toward unbelievers, but Paul is pleading
with believers and so mentions their conduct among them.
The Thessalonians know of the consistency of the lives of
the missionaries.

[11] Again Paul appeals to the knowledge of the readers for confirmation of the conduct of the missionaries. That
which the Thessalonians know is that the evangelists had
exhorted, encouraged, and charged them **like a father with
his children.** Attention to individuals is implied by the
expression **each one of you.** Exhorting, encouraging, and
charging give emphasis to the teaching that was done; thus
the change of comparison from that of a nursing mother
(vs. 7) to that of a **father** is very appropriate. The evangelists had manifested the affection and earnestness of a sincere and pious father exhorting his own children. They
were concerned; they cared as a father cares. Deep feeling
is expressed in this comparison (cf. 1 Cor. 4:14ff.).

The activities of exhorting, encouraging, and charging
suggest different phases in the teaching ministry. **Exhorted**
indicates the pleading and the admonishing which were
done by the evangelists (cf. 2 Cor. 5:20 where the word is
translated "beseeching"). **Encouraged** or comforted evidently refers to speaking words of consolation and encouragement to those who were experiencing difficulty in living
the Christian life in the midst of severe opposition (cf.
5:14). **Charged** has within it the idea of solemn declaration
of serious words. In 4:6 Paul reminds the Thessalonians of

47

¹² to lead a life worthy of God, who calls you into his
kingdom and glory.

---

one particular instance in which this type of teaching had
been done. The three words (participles in the Greek)
present a more thorough description of the conduct of the
preachers toward the Thessalonians. At times a father exhorts and encourages his children; at times he addresses
them in terms more severe. In these ways Paul and his helpers had spoken to the Thessalonians.

[12] The purpose or aim of the actions denoted by the
three participles was that the Thessalonians might **lead a
life worthy of God.** The expression, **lead a life,** comes from
a Greek word which literally means "to walk." The same
expression is found in 4:1 where it is translated "to live."
The Christian life as a walk is a favorite image with Paul
(e.g., see Rom. 8:4; 13:13; 1 Cor. 7:17; 2 Cor. 5:7; Gal. 5:16;
Eph. 4:17; 5:15; Col. 4:5). Paul also uses the imagery in
describing a manner of life other than the Christian life
(e.g., 1 Cor. 3:3; 2 Cor. 4:2; Phil. 3:18; Col. 3:7). The
expression, **worthy of God,** describes a life in which man
offers to God the very best that he can; it involves the
surrendering of man's will to God's will. No higher standard can be contemplated than that of leading a life worthy
of God. The principal idea seems to be that of leading a life
that is in harmony with the Christian's relation to God. It is
in this same sense that Paul exhorts the Ephesians "to lead
a life worthy of the calling to which you have been called"
(Eph. 4:1). He is urging them to lead lives that are consist-
ent with their profession. Paul never thinks of man being
worthy of God in the absolute sense, that is, insofar as his
own meritorious achievements are concerned; he does contemplate the goal of being "counted worthy" upon the
merits of Christ (see notes on 2 Thess. 1:5). He exhorts
Christians to live "worthy of the gospel," that is, in harmony with it (Phil. 1:27). He prayed that the Colossians
might "lead a life worthy of the Lord" (Col. 1:10). How-

¹³ And we also thank God constantly for this, that when you received the word of God which you heard from us, you accepted it not as the word of men but as what it really is, the word of God, which is at work in you believers.

---

ever, in the same prayer he asked that they might continue to increase in knowledge; this indicates that he did not consider walking worthily to be a state of absolute perfection. Furthermore, in the same prayer he asks that the Colossians "be strengthened with all might," showing that God is the source of their power to walk worthily.

The participial clause, who calls you into his own kingdom and glory, is descriptive of God. The present participle indicates the continual calling of God. Kingdom and glory are objects of the same preposition and only one definite article is used with the two words; kingdom and glory are thus seen to be very closely related. During the personal ministry of Christ the sons of Zebedee came to him asking for prominent positions "in your kingdom" (Matt. 20:21). However, in the parallel passage the expression is "in your glory" (Mk. 10:37). Christians are in the kingdom of God now. Paul declares that God "has delivered us from the dominion of darkness and transferred us to the kingdom of his beloved Son" (Col. 1:13). Likewise, there is a sense in which Christians in this life see the glory of the Lord (2 Cor. 3:18). However, the ultimate end of God's redemptive work is that men might have "an entrance into the eternal kingdom of our Lord and Savior Jesus Christ" (2 Peter 1:11) and that "When Christ who is our life appears," they too "will appear with him in glory" (Col. 3:4; cf. 1 Peter 5:10). The fullest realization of that into which Christians are being called is yet future.

Response to the Message, 2:13–16

[13] Having discussed the nature of their ministry in Thessalonica, the writers now resume the thanksgiving of 1:2ff. In the Greek this section is introduced by a consecu-

tive, subordinating expression which evidently looks back
over the entire previous section of chapter 2. Some (e.g.,
Frame and Milligan) think the **and** indicates reciprocal
thanksgiving—that likely Paul had received news from the
Thessalonians regarding their thanksgiving for having received the gospel and he now expresses thanksgiving in
return. This may well have been the case. The use of the
emphatic Greek pronoun *hēmeis,* **we,** gives strength to this
idea. Whatever the case, Paul wants his readers to know
that, though he and his helpers are absent from their Thessalonian brethren, they never cease being thankful for them
and for the attitude they had manifested toward the
gospel.

With the word **that** Paul introduces a clause which sets
forth the ground for the thanksgiving just expressed. The
temporal expression, **when you received the word of God
which you heard from us,** refers to the external act of
receiving. The outward and objective hearing is in Paul's
mind. **Of God** (subjective genitive) gives emphasis to the
fact that the word or message originated from God. Paul
thus views God as the ultimate source of the message and
himself and his helpers as the instruments through which
the message came to the Thessalonians; they were "servants
through whom" the Thessalonians came to believe (see 1
Cor. 3:5; cf. 2 Cor. 5:20ff.).

Paul goes further in his thanksgiving. The Thessalonians
not only had **received** (Greek, *paralambanō*) the word in
the sense of giving it a hearing; they had **accepted** it. The
Greek verb *dechomai* indicates that they had welcomed
that which they had heard (cf. Heb. 4:2 as an instance of
an opposite response). Paul finds ground for thanksgiving
both negatively and positively: negatively in the fact that
the Thessalonians had not received **the word of men** and
positively in the fact that they had received the message for
what it was—**the word of God.** Men were the agents
through whom the word was brought but they were not its
source (cf. Gal. 1:11ff.). The RSV (and others) inserts the

¹⁴ For you, brethren, became imitators of the churches of
God in Christ Jesus which are in Judea; for you suffered
the same things from your own countrymen as they did
from the Jews,

---

word as before the expression, **the word of men.** However,
the word as is not in the original. Its insertion at this point
is unnecessary. The declaration, "You accepted not a message of man," describes more forcibly the character of the
message to which reference is made. The Thessalonians
had not accepted a message of man but that which was
truly the word of God. Paul was conscious of inspiration.
He recognized the divine origin of his message. He here
expresses his gratitude that the hearers had not been de-
luded in any way as to the nature of the message. They had
recognized it as the inspired word of God.

Paul describes the word of God as that **which is at work
in you believers. Believers** is a term used by Paul to designate Christians. The word of God had been powerful in the
lives of these people when it was first heard. The gospel "is
the power of God for salvation" (Rom. 1:16). That same
word continues its efficacy in the lives of Christians. Paul
here employs the present tense, **is at work,** pointing to the
continued activity of the word of God in the hearts of the
Thessalonians. The word has energizing power and serves
to bring forth Christian graces (cf. Eph. 3:20; Phil. 2:12ff.).
One particular grace which the word of God produces is
patience, and Paul elaborates upon that grace further in
discussing the severe persecutions which the Thessalonians
had recently endured.

[14] With the word **for** Paul proceeds to give confirmation of the continued activity of the energizing word in the
lives of the Thessalonians. He states the historical fact
concerning the Thessalonians having become **imitators of**
the Judean churches. **Churches of God** is an expression
indicating ownership (cf. Gal. 1:22; Rom. 16:16). These
churches are further described as being **in Christ Jesus,**

indicating spiritual union with him. **In Judea** gives the
geographical location of these churches. The Thessalonian
church had imitated these churches in a way that was most
commendable, and the specific point of imitation which
Paul specifies is this: the Thessalonians had suffered for
their faith at the hands of their fellow-citizens just as the
Christians in Judea had suffered for their faith at the hands
of their fellow-Jews. In 1:6 Paul praised the Thessalonians
highly because they had become "imitators" of the missionaries and of the Lord in the way they had "received the
word in much affliction, with joy inspired by the Holy
Spirit." The Greek word *mimētai*, from which our word
"imitators" comes, has within it the idea of a mimic, signifying more than a follower. It indicates a reproduction of
attitude and of conduct which has been in others. The word
occurs six times in the New Testament; the other four
occurrences are 1 Corinthians 4:16; 11:1; Ephesians 5:1;
and Hebrews 6:12.

It is evident that the **own countrymen** of the Thessalonians were predominantly Gentiles. However, persecution
against Paul and his helpers in Thessalonica had been
instigated by the Jews (Acts 17:5-7); it is likely that Jewish
hatred was still at the bottom of Gentile persecution. This is
perhaps one reason for Paul's reference to Jewish persecution. The Judean churches had existed for quite some time
and the persecutions they had endured were well known
over a wide area. Jewish persecution of the Judean
churches is a prominent subject in the early chapters of
Acts. The Christians of that region had endured in the
midst of afflictions. Paul's comparison of the Thessalonian
Christians with the Christians of Judea is thus seen to be
quite meaningful. It is also a fact that Paul sees the Jews as
a perpetual threat to the cause of righteousness. Throughout his own ministry Paul had met opposition from them.
This fact is seen in the historical references in Acts and is
reflected in such epistles as 2 Corinthians, Galatians, and
Philippians.

¹⁵ **who killed both the Lord Jesus and the prophets, and drove us out, and displease God and oppose all men**

---

[15] Paul now launches into a bitter denunciation of the persecuting Jews; he evidences a bitterness that is unparalleled in any of his other writings. This is quite understandable when the Jewish efforts to thwart his evangelistic plans are taken into account; when their determined effort to undermine Paul's influence is considered; and when their persistent efforts to destroy churches which Paul had established are remembered. Now, in a series of four participial clauses Paul sets forth the true character of these persecutors.

The first two clauses used by Paul to describe the persecuting Jews refer to events in the past: **who killed both the Lord Jesus and the prophets and drove us out**. The heinous act of crucifying their Messiah was the crowning sin of the Jewish nation. "By the hands of lawless men" they had "crucified and killed" Jesus the Lord (Acts 2:23). However, in killing the Messiah they were not acting out of character, for their long history had shown opposition to the messengers of God. Jesus himself, while on earth, addressed Jerusalem as a city that had killed the prophets and stoned those who had been sent to her (Matt. 23:37). In irony he had said, "It cannot be that a prophet should perish away from Jerusalem" (Luke 13:33ff.). Stephen accused the Jews of his day of doing as their fathers had done and he asked, "Which of the prophets did not your fathers persecute?" (Acts 7:51, 52). The expression, **drove us out**, evidently has reference to the treatment which had been suffered by Paul, Silvanus, and Timothy in Thessalonica and in Beroea. In Thessalonica the jealous Jews brought Jason and certain other brethren before the city authorities, making false and absurd accusations against Paul and his helpers. They were not able to locate Paul and his companions whom the brethren immediately sent out of the city. These same determined Jewish persecutors heard of Paul's preaching in

¹⁶ **by hindering us from speaking to the Gentiles that they
may be saved—so as always to fill up the measure of their
sins. But God's wrath has come upon them at last!** ᵇ

ᵇ Or *completely,* or *for ever*

Beroea and pursued him there, "stirring up and inciting the
crowds." So, once again Paul is sent away by the brethren;
in a real sense it could be said that he was driven out by the
Jews (Acts 17:5-14).

The next two participial clauses refer to the present,
constant attitude of the Jews: **displease God and oppose all
men.** Paul employs present participles indicating an habitual and continuous attitude which causes God to be dis-
pleased with these Jews. Further, Paul declares that they
oppose all men. This terse statement epitomizes their constant and bitter opposition to the work of the gospel emissaries. In opposing the preaching of the gospel they were
hindering that which alone could bring salvation to men of
every race. In this way they were arraying themselves
against the salvation of all men. Paul's accusation here
against the Jews seems to be more restricted, as verse 16
will bear out, than the references found in Tacitus and
other writers to the Jewish hatred and hostility toward all
other men.

[16] In an explanatory clause Paul more clearly defines
what he means by the expression, **oppose all men.** The
contrary attitude toward all men possessed by the Jews was
manifested **by hindering us from speaking to the Gentiles
that they may be saved.** Like the Pharisees of whom Jesus
spoke, they were not content to remain outside the kingdom; they insisted on keeping others out also (Matt.
23:13). The violent rejection of the gospel by the Jews had
reached its height in their determination that the gospel
should not be brought to the Gentiles (cf. Acts 14:1ff.).
That they may be saved describes more fully the speaking
which the Jews were determined to prevent. It was not
mere speaking to the Gentiles that the Jews were so stren-

uously trying to prevent; it was that speaking which had as
its purpose the salvation of the Gentiles. They were determined to prevent others from enjoying that salvation which
they themselves so persistently scorned. Paul can vividly
remember the envious actions of the Jews against him while
he was in Thessalonica, the incident which aroused the
entire city (Acts 17:5). Paul also experienced great opposition from the unbelieving Jews in Corinth, the place from
which this epistle is being written (Acts 18:6ff.). However,
he wrote soon after Timothy arrived in Corinth, and it is
not known to what extent the opposition existed at the time
of the writing of 1 Thessalonians (see notes on 3:6).

The expression, **so as always to fill up the measure of
their sins,** indicates that the Jews of whom Paul is speaking
are continuing to do as their fathers had always done. In
addition to killing the prophets, crucifying the Lord, and
persecuting the apostles, they have set themselves against
the salvation of all men. The Jews have always been adding
to the measure of their sins, have been engaged in the
activity of filling up the measure full; they are still engaged
in such activity, says Paul.

There are those who see in the expression, **to fill up the
measure of their sins,** the idea of purpose. This is the usual
significance of the Greek construction. Ellicott sees it as
purpose and to be connected not only with **hindering** but
with the whole of verse 15. From a grammatical viewpoint,
Ellicott says the purpose is to be attributed to the Jews. He
points out that their actions might be seen as intentional
and conscious or that the Jews might be regarded as
blinded, yet acting as agents. However, along with the
grammatical construction, Ellicott sees in the purpose idea
the intention of God which was being unfolded in the
wilful blindness of his people. Milligan follows the same
line of reasoning and alleges that Romans 1:20, 24; 4:11 are
other instances in which the same Greek construction denotes a purpose contemplated by God and not by the one
performing the particular act. Frame says that all that the

persecuting Jews have done was done with the purpose of
filling up their sins. However, he says the purpose is to be
understood as that of God and not of the Jews themselves.
He sees Jewish obstinacy as an item in the overall plan of
God. Frame says the idea underlying **to fill up** is found in
certain passages in the Septuagint as Genesis 15:16, Daniel
8:23, and 2 Maccabees 6:14. These passages portray God as
waiting until certain transgressors have reached the full
measure or the state of completeness of their sins. Morris
sees the determined obstinacy of the Jews in the passage
and points out that they are making certain that no sin is
omitted from their long history of opposition to the plan of
God. He also sees Jewish obstinacy as an element in the
plan of God.

There is the probability that nothing more than result is
intended by the expression, **so as always to fill up the
measure of their sins.** Robertson agrees that it could have
been the conceived plan of God to allow the Jews to go
ahead and fill up the measure of sins or that the expression
may describe the normal consequence which came from the
continual sins of the nation. Lenski grants that the idea of
God's wanting the Jews to go ahead and run the full course
in their sins is true—that God permits the one who casts off
all restraints and plunges into excess to go ahead and fill up
the measure of his sins until he is destroyed. However,
Lenski prefers to think of result as being in Paul's mind in
the present passage. He calls attention to the idea of result
in the next clause pertaining to wrath and points out that
the result which the Jews had always been attaining by
their sins more definitely fits the idea of result than that of
purpose. Lightfoot says that 2 Corinthians 8:6 and probably Hebrews 11:3 are instances of *eis* with the articular
infinitive indicating consequence. He maintains that, this
being the case, one cannot insist that Paul, in the present
passage, is indicating that the Jews had the conscious intention of filling up the measure of their sins. Moreover, Lightfoot says that one cannot insist that Paul had in mind the

fact that God's purpose was overruling the actions of the Jews. However, he agrees that the latter idea is not improbable when viewed from either a grammatical or a theological standpoint.

Without doubt, it is true that the Jews had been obstinate and wilfully blind (Matt. 13:14, 15; Acts 7:51-53). They had often acted in ignorance (Lk. 23:34; Acts 3:17; Rom. 10:3). True, their ignorance was wilful and was due to their obstinacy. But it would be difficult to say to what extent they knowingly and with purpose filled up the measure of their sins. It is also true that it has been a part of the overall divine plan to let a people go on in their rebellion until their sin is complete. To the scribes and Pharisees of his day, Jesus said, "Fill up, then, the measure of your fathers" (Matt. 23:32; cf. the entire passage, Matt. 23:29-36). Jesus is thus permitting them to go ahead in their course of bringing to completion the rebellion which had been begun by their forefathers. He sees their state of mind and their determined course of action. Though it is contrary to his wishes, he permits them to go ahead and fill up the measure. In this sense can such procedure be viewed as fitting into the overall framework of the purpose of God. Too, without doubt, the natural result of the persistent conduct of the Jews is accurately described in the passage under consideration. Was Paul intending to indicate purpose or result? Decision is difficult. Perhaps in Paul's thinking there is not always a great distinction between the two. The general teaching of the passage is not greatly affected, regardless of the route one takes. One could not in fairness insist absolutely upon either to the complete exclusion of the other.

The statement, **but God's wrath has come upon them at last,** denotes the strong contrast between the conduct of the Jews and its result. In what way does Paul think of the **wrath** of God as having already **come upon** (past tense in Greek) the Jews? There is the possibility that he indicates the certainty of an approaching event. Some, as Ellicott, think Paul is pointing to the wrath of God which was to descend upon the nation at the fall of Jerusalem in A.D. 70, an event that was not far distant in the future at the time of the writing of this epistle. Others, as Morris, feel that Paul is thinking of the wrath of God which will fall upon the nation at the end of time—eschatological wrath. They see in the tense used the certainty of the event. This may be the case. Or it may be that Paul is thinking of God's wrath having come in the sense that his displeasure is evoked and that he looks to the future for the execution of that wrath. In 1:10 Paul speaks of "the wrath to come." In Romans 1:18 he says that "the wrath of God is revealed from heaven," while in Romans 2:5 he clearly looks to "the day of wrath when God's righteous judgment will be revealed." In some sense Paul saw God's wrath as having already fallen. This does not mean that he denied the continuance of that wrath nor its eschatological phase. To be sure, God's wrath will be evident at the end of time.

The expression, at last, comes from a Greek construction which is variously translated. It is translated "to the very last" (Josh. 8:24); "complete" (2 Chron. 12:12); "always" (Ps. 9:18); "to the end" (Matt. 10:22); "continual" (Luke 18:5). God's patience, so long manifested toward the nation, has at last been exhausted. His wrath, long withheld, has now been manifested. The nation has fallen under the blow of divine retribution. It may be that Paul is looking forward to the destruction of Jerusalem as a time of the display of the wrath of God; or it may be that he is thinking in terms of the judgment day; or it may be that he was thinking both of the last day and of the day of Jerusalem's downfall, an event which would in a way foreshadow the final day of judgment. Jesus described in vivid language the end of the Jewish nation (Matt. 24:3ff.). Paul elsewhere (cf. Rom. 11) spoke at length of God's rejection of Israel. However, there is likely no equal anywhere in the New Testament to the severity expressed in verses 15 and 16 of the present chapter.

¹⁷ But since we were bereft of you, brethren, for a short time, in person not in heart, we endeavored the more eagerly and with great desire to see you face to face;

Paul's Continued Interest, 2:17-20

[17] By the use of an adversative conjunction and an emphatic personal pronoun Paul now proceeds to contrast himself and his friends with the Jewish persecutors. It is possible that critics at Thessalonica had said that Paul never had any intention of returning and that his continued absence indicated that he had forgotten the Thessalonian Christians. It will be remembered that a similar charge was later made against Paul by enemies at Corinth (2 Cor. 1:15ff.). Such an idea was, of course, absurd. Paul had a very strong feeling for the churches he established. It was his custom of keeping in contact with a newly established church either by means of letter, or messengers, or by personal visits.

Here, in the strongest possible terms, Paul affirms the desire of himself and his helpers to see the Thessalonians **in person.** He says that they had been **bereft of** the Thessalonians, a word that means being orphaned. This adds another note of tender affection to that contained in the ideas of a nurse caring for her children and of the conduct of a father toward his children—ideas used earlier in the chapter. Paul often changes imagery. In the figure now under discussion he thinks of himself and his helpers as being orphaned by their absence from their brethren in Thessalonica. Feeling bereft or orphaned, they desired **to see** the Thessalonians. This strong desire was felt even after they had been separated from them only **for a short time.** The separation or absence is described both positively and negatively: it was an absence only **in person;** it was **not** an absence **in heart.** The Thessalonians had continued to have a warm place in the hearts of the missionaries though they

[18] because we wanted to come to you—I, Paul, again and again—but Satan hindered us.

were physically separated from them. And all of the time they were longing to see them **face to face.** **We endeavored** is a strong verb indicating intense earnestness. The comparative adverb which is tranlated **the more eagerly** reenforces the strength of the verb. The prepositional phrase, **with great desire,** indicates intense desire, a fierce longing. Paul's use of all these, together with the affectionate **brethren,** is strongly indicative of the great love shared by the missionaries for the Thessalonian Christians (cf. 3:10).

[18] Introducing the thought with **because,** Paul reaffirms the fact that he and his companions did wish **to see** the Thessalonians. They had a fervent desire to come to them. Paul adds his own name in what might be called an emphatic singular: **I Paul.** The singular stands out as emphatic over against the many plurals in the epistle. Paul wants the Thessalonians to know that he, personally, has the wish he is here describing. This desire had not been felt only on a certain occasion, but had been felt **again and again.**

But Satan hindered us is Paul's explanation of why he and his colleagues had not visited the Thessalonians as they had desired to do. Though the desire had been keen and constant, circumstances hindered its being carried out. Various conjectures could be made as to the nature of the hindrance. Lightfoot thinks the most plausible conjecture is that Paul is referring to Jewish opposition. However, it is futile to inquire as to the exact nature of the hindrance. Whatever the means involved, Paul recognized the hindrance as the work of Satan. Anything which hinders God's messengers from doing the work of the kingdom may rightly be viewed as the work of Satan (cf. Job 1:6ff.; Zech. 3:1; Matt. 4:10; Mark 4:15; Lk. 22:3; 22:31; Acts 5:3; Rom. 16:20; 1 Cor. 5:5; 7:5; 2 Cor. 2:11; 11:14; 12:7; 2 Thess. 2:9).

¹⁹ For what is our hope or joy or crown of boasting before
our Lord Jesus at his coming? Is it not you?

---

[19] With for Paul introduces the motive for the ardent
desire on the part of himself and his helpers to return to
Thessalonica. These missionaries include their friends there
in their highest hopes: they are a source of deep joy; they
are to them a crown of boasting. The word crown denoted
something like a garland or a wreath which was awarded to
victorious athletes. Crown of boasting or "of glorying" has
reference to the outward expression of the feeling of inward joy over these converts who have remained loyal in
the face of severe opposition. Paul addressed the Philippians as "my joy and crown" (Phil. 4:1). However, he exhorts
them to hold "fast the word of life, so that in the day of
Christ I may be proud that I did not run in vain or labor in
vain" (Phil. 2:16). He is thinking of the judgment day
when Christ will reward his servants. He wants his converts
to be faithful to the end so that he may take pride in them;
they will be proof that his hard labors were not wasted—
were not in vain. They will be thus his crown of boasting or
of rejoicing. Similarly, he has had fears that Satan may
cause the Thessalonians to fall and that thus his labors
among the Thessalonians would be "in vain." Paul uses the
expression "in vain" as the antithesis to the expression
"crown of boasting." In one case he feared that his converts
would not stand in the judgment day as loyal disciples in
whom he could rejoice; in the other he envisions them as
his crown of boasting, proof of the fruitfulness of his
ministry.

Paul designates the coming (*parousia*) of Jesus as the
day when the hope, joy, and crown will find full realization.
The coming of Christ was mentioned at the close of chapter
one of this epistle. However, here is the first instance in
Christian literature of this important word, *parousia.*
Thayer points out that in the ordinary language of the people
the word had special application to the arrival of an im-

²⁰ For you are our glory and joy.

portant person. Paul uses the word regarding the arrival of one of his trusted helpers (2 Cor. 7:6). It was the usual word pertaining to a royal visit. In the New Testament it became the technical expression for the second coming of Christ. It is derived from the word *pareimi* which means "I am beside" or "I am alongside." It can well be translated either by the word coming or by the word "presence." Paul uses the word four times in 1 Thessalonians and each time with reference to the second coming of Christ (2:19; 3:13; 4:15; 5:23). Paul writes with absolute certainty regarding the return of Christ. In fact, Paul eagerly anticipated and longed for the *parousia*.

[20] Concern and compassion for their converts are seen in the words of the writers. These feelings leap out again and again (cf. 2 Thess. 1:4). The writers conclude this section by assuring the Thessalonians that they themselves are their glory and their joy. The present tense, you are, shows the continuing reality of this meaningful feeling. Even though Paul and his helpers look forward with anticipation to the *parousia* as the time of the full realization of glory and hope, still they can affirm that, at the very time of writing, the Thessalonians are their glory and joy. There could be no material possession comparable with this. The exceedingly strong affection for the Thessalonian Christians expressed by the writers in this chapter would be of a most encouraging nature to the readers of the epistle. And if, as some things seem to indicate, there were slanderous reports being circulated about the missionaries by enemies in Thessalonica, the strong assurances of this chapter would go a long way toward refuting such reports.

The Mission of Timothy to Thessalonica, 3:1–5

The writers began their discussion of the personal interest they felt in the Thessalonians in 2:17; they employed rather strong language to describe this interest which they

¹ Therefore when we could bear it no longer, we were willing to be left behind at Athens alone,

---

felt, even while absent. Paul himself assures the Thessalonians that he had tried to visit them again and again and he assures them that they are his hope, joy, and crown. As evidence of their deep concern, Paul and his helpers continue the discussion of their personal interest in the Thessalonians throughout chapter 3.

[1] The sending of Timothy to the Thessalonian church is presented as another evidence of the deep solicitation felt by Paul and his co-laborers. In Luke's record of the travels of the missionaries he relates that Paul instructed the Bereans who had accompanied him to Athens to return to Beroea and to send Timothy and Silas to him at Athens (Acts 17:15). Evidently Paul wanted both Silvanus and Timothy to accompany him to Corinth; however, he was not able to take either of them (Acts 18:5). Upon the arrival of Silvanus and Timothy at Athens it was agreed that Timothy would return to Thessalonica. Just how long Silvanus remained with Paul after Timothy's departure for Thessalonica is not known. At some subsequent time he went into Macedonia. Because of the absence of details in Acts it is difficult to reconstruct with accuracy the actions of the missionaries. It is known, however, that eventually both Silvanus and Timothy rejoined Paul while he was in Corinth and that they came from Macedonia (Acts 18:5).

Therefore, having a consecutive significance, sums up the principal points of 2:17-20. It was after Paul and his helpers had been absent from Thessalonica for a short time and after their intense desire to visit Thessalonica had been thwarted by Satan that the decision to send Timothy was made.

The clause, when we could bear it no longer, is a participial clause in the Greek and is best construed as causal. It states a fact which motivated the action taken.

² and we sent Timothy, our brother and God's servant in
the gospel of Christ, to establish you in your faith and to
exhort you,

Satan had frustrated the immediate plans of the missionaries to return to Thessalonica, but their intense yearning
was not thereby quenched. Finally, after bearing the pain
and anguish until it was unbearable, Paul and Silvanus
were willing to be left in **Athens alone** in order that Timothy might visit the Thessalonians. The word from which
alone comes is plural in the Greek, indicating that Paul
meant to include Silvanus along with himself. The word
from which **to be left behind** comes is a strong word and is
sometimes used to describe being left behind by the death
of a loved one (e.g., Luke 20:31). The emphatic word,
alone, augments the emotional content of the verb. This
shows how deeply Paul and Silvanus missed the presence of
Timothy. The nature of the city in which they were left
alone would further deepen their sense of loneliness. Of all
the cities visited by Paul, Athens was likely the most trying
to his keen sensitivity. It was a city that was deeply religious, being filled with idols, and yet it must have seemed
to Paul more distantly alienated from God than any other
city of the world of his day.

[2] The description Paul gives of Timothy indicates
something of the high type of character of this traveling
companion of Paul and also something of the high regard in
which Paul held him. **Our brother** is a very affectionate
term. **God's servant** is highly complimentary. The Greek
has "fellow worker of God." The term denotes that Timothy
was not a worker with other missionaries but with God.
The prepositional phrase, **in the gospel of Christ,** designates
the sphere in which Timothy works with God. Timothy was
quite young at this time; he did not have a great deal of
experience in this type of work, having joined the missionary group earlier on the second tour (Acts 16:1-3). Later,
writing to the Philippians, Paul again highly compliments

Timothy and gives a further insight into the type of work with which he entrusted him (Phil. 2:19-24).

It is evident that Paul wishes, by this high and sincere tribute to Timothy, to give emphasis to the sacrifice which was made by himself and Silvanus in being deprived of his company. He is still desirous of impressing upon the minds of the Thessalonians their deep concern for them. It is also likely that Paul wishes to exalt Timothy in the estimation of the Thessalonians and thus to silence any possible complaint that it was Timothy rather than Paul who was coming to them. It is not known just why Timothy was the one selected to go to Thessalonica. Ellicott suggests that it was likely that Timothy, having been able to obey Paul's orders to come to Athens more quickly than Silvanus, was sent at once to Thessalonica before the arrival of Silvanus in Athens. However, this is ruled out if Silvanus cooperated in the sending of Timothy, and the use of the plural strongly favors the inclusion of Silvanus. Findlay suggests that Timothy may have been sent due to the fact that he was not marked out for attack in Thessalonica in the same way as were the others and that he could return when they could not. There is no way of knowing for certain why Timothy was the one sent.

Paul states the purpose for the sending of Timothy: **to establish you in your faith and to exhort you.** The word from which **establish** comes means "to make stable," "to strengthen," or "to confirm." The word translated **exhort** has also the meaning "to comfort." Timothy, then, was to confirm the Thessalonians in their present manner of life and he was to speak to them in such a way that they would be comforted in their afflictions and encouraged to renewed efforts. Where the RSV has **in your faith** the Greek has literally "in behalf of your faith." Timothy's visit was thus intended to be to the advantage of the faith of the Thessalonians. He was to strengthen their faith and encourage them in such a way as to benefit or promote their faith. Paul's repeated use of the word "faith" in his two letters to

65

³ that no one be moved by these afflictions. You yourselves know that this is to be our lot. ⁴ For when we were with you, we told you beforehand that we were to suffer affliction; just as it has come to pass, and as you know.

---

the Thessalonians shows his deep concern about the faith of these young Christians (e.g., 1 Thess. 1:3, 8; 3:5, 6, 7; 5:8; 2 Thess. 1:3, 4, 11).

[3] **To establish** and **to exhort** of the preceding verse state the primary purpose for the sending of Timothy. But a secondary purpose which in reality is dependent upon the accomplishment of the primary one is **that no one be moved by these afflictions.** The verb from which **moved** is translated originally meant "to fawn upon," or "to flatter," or "to wag the tail." Paul has the fear that certain false teachers might, with flattery, in a gesture of pretended friendliness, as a dog might wag its tail when seeking friendship, move the Thessalonians away from their faith. Timothy was sent in order that he might establish and encourage them in order to prevent any such false deception by false teachers. **By these afflictions** or "in these afflictions" designates the sphere in which the Thessalonians are living the Christian life. The fact that they are living in the midst of such afflictions intensifies Paul's fears that they might be beguiled.

Paul goes ahead to remind the Thessalonians that they **know that this is to be our lot.** Christians are certain to encounter opposition in this world. The antithesis between good and evil is such that the good will always find the forces of hostility pitted against it. Jesus said, "If you were of the world, the world would love its own; but because you are not of the world, but I chose you out of the world, therefore the world hates you" (John 15:19; cf. Acts 14:22; 2 Tim. 3:12).

[4] With the introductory **for** Paul further explains his statement of verse 3. The Thessalonians had no reason to be surprised over the sufferings they were enduring. Paul

had, when in their midst, forewarned that this was something they could expect. The expression, **we told you beforehand,** is from a verb which literally translated would be, "we were telling you before." The force of the Greek tense is that Paul and his companions had told them repeatedly over a period of time. It was not a matter which they had mentioned only once. That of which they had repeatedly warned the Thessalonians was that **we were to suffer affliction.** Literally rendered, this would be "we are about to be afflicted." Paul knew that becoming a Christian did not exempt a person from hardship. Indeed, he knew that in some respects it would involve additional hardships to which the unbeliever is a stranger. He also knew that God had a purpose in permitting Christians to suffer, that there is a redemptive aspect to sufferings. He knew that out of the trials and afflictions of life is born the kind of character which God is seeking to develop. It was due to this realization that he could say, "More than that, we rejoice in our sufferings, knowing that suffering produces endurance, and endurance produces character, and character produces hope" (Rom. 5:3, 4).

As Paul now writes to the Thessalonian Christians, he can say, **just as it has come to pass, and as you know.** In these two comparative clauses Paul is saying that the sufferings which he had foretold had occurred just as he said they would and that the Thessalonians, because of their experience in these sufferings, can testify to their reality. Often in the epistle Paul by the words, "you know," appeals to the Thessalonians in confirmation of the truthfulness of what he is writing. It could very well be that in this appeal Paul not only intends to encourage the readers in their trials, but that he also intends to refute insinuations from enemies to the effect that persecutions or any kind of suffering which a Christian might undergo was proof that the religion which he had espoused was, after all, a delusion. Paul had never promised Christians exemption from trials; on the contrary, he had repeatedly told them that it was a

⁵ For this reason, when I could bear it no longer, I sent that I might know your faith, for fear that somehow the tempter had tempted you and that our labor would be in vain.

---

part of the divine arrangement that Christians should have such trials.

[5] Paul now returns to the subject of verses 1, 2, the earnest care of the writers and the sending of Timothy to Thessalonica. However, in contrast with the plurals of verses 1, 2, Paul now employs the emphatic first person singular. It seems that he desires to emphasize in a special way his own personal care and anxiety and that he wants the Thessalonians to know that he had personally taken the lead in the sending of Timothy. Hence he says, **when I could bear it no longer, I sent. . . .** If it be true that charges were being made in Thessalonica, it is likely that enemies would make Paul the special target of their criticism, alleging that he had deserted the converts and had no intention of returning to them. It may be that such charges caused Paul to write of his own actions with such emphasis. The unbearable suspense which resulted in the sending of Timothy, mentioned before in verse 1, is here repeated by Paul.

In the restatement of the thought of verses 1, 2, the unbearable suspense and the sending of Timothy to Thessalonica, Paul now adds an additional purpose which he had in mind in the sending of Timothy: **that I might know your faith.** He knows that the faith of new converts is a crucial matter. He desired that Timothy see the Christians in Thessalonica, observe them in their daily conduct, and learn by personal contact something of their **faith.** Paul desired a firsthand report from Timothy in order that he might come to have a knowledge of the state of their faith.

Paul has a fear that **the tempter had tempted** the Christians in Thessalonica. The participle which is here translated "the tempter" literally means "the one tempting," and brings out most forcefully the characteristic work of Satan.

⁶ But now that Timothy has come to us from you, and has brought us the good news of your faith and love and reported that you always remember us kindly and long to see us, as we long to see you—

Only in one other passage (Matt. 4:3) is Satan thus designated in the New Testament. Previously in this epistle (2:18) Paul has spoken of Satan's hindering his plans to return to Thessalonica. It is nothing unusual for Paul to make mention of this foe. He spoke of his thorn in the flesh as "a messenger of Satan" (2 Cor. 12:2). He spoke of preventing Satan "from gaining the advantage over us," and then said, "for we are not ignorant of his designs" (2 Cor. 2:11). Paul believed that in the person of Satan, **the tempter,** Christians have a great and dangerous spiritual enemy who is bent on frustrating the work of God (see notes on 2:18). By **our labor** Paul has reference to the hard work which he, Silvanus, and Timothy had expended in behalf of the Thessalonians when they were with them. When he adds the phrase **would be in vain,** he suggests the possible outcome of the temptations to which his readers were being exposed and would continue to be exposed. On the expression "in vain" see notes on 2:1 and 2:19 (cf. Phil. 2:16; Gal. 2:2; 4:11).

Joy over the News Brought by Timothy, 3:6–10

[6] An exuberance of happiness is evident in this section. Having described how the writers, Paul in particular, had felt at the time they sent Timothy on his mission to Thessalonica, the writers go on to describe their state of mind now that Timothy has returned to them. They give a brief but rather complete report of the news conveyed by Timothy. The fact that **Timothy has come to us from you** is prefaced by the word **now.** The word could well be translated "just now." It strictly denotes present time as contrasted with past or future time. It seems that by the use of the word Paul wishes to add another item to show his

intense interest and concern. He is writing at the very moment, so to speak, that Timothy arrived with the news. A delay in writing might indicate a lack of concern. **From you** indicates the source of the news Paul desires to hear, the Thessalonians themselves.

Paul says that Timothy **has brought us the good news.** The expression is interesting for the words, **has brought . . . the good news** is from a single Greek word. The word conveys the idea of bringing good news but it is a word that is not elsewhere used by Paul in a sense other than to denote gospel preaching. Paul's use of the word in this unusual sense is an indication of the joy he feels over the news brought by Timothy, news which was indeed a veritable gospel.

The first element in the good news which Timothy brings concerns the **faith** of the Thessalonians. Paul has said that he sent Timothy to establish the Thessalonians in their faith (vs. 2); he has also said that he sent Timothy for the purpose of knowing about their faith (vs. 5). Now, concerning the **faith** of these people, Timothy brings a most favorable report.

The second element in the good news which Timothy brings concerns the **love** of the Thessalonians. Just what Timothy reported concerning their love is not revealed. The fact that Paul considered it good news shows that it was favorable. Faith and love constitute a fairly good epitome of true Christian character, and where the two exist there will also be found the fruits which God expects. "For in Christ Jesus neither circumcision nor uncircumcision is of any avail, but faith working through love" (Gal. 5:6). Where true faith and true love exist the fruitful works of faith will be evident (see 1 John 3:23). It is no wonder that Paul's heart overflows with joy over the good report concerning these two significant attributes.

A third item in the report brought by Timothy which gives Paul much satisfaction is that the Thessalonians continue to have a good remembrance of Paul and his helpers.

⁷ for this reason, brethren, in all our distress and affliction
we have been comforted about you through your faith;

Timothy has reported that you always remember us kindly,
says Paul. The Thessalonians had been remembering the
missionaries with fondness and had been doing so always.
The constancy of their kind remembrance is thus emphasized. Paul had entertained fears that the opposition of the
hostile Jews might cause the Thessalonians to think less of
the missionaries and to hold them in light esteem. But the
Thessalonians, says Timothy, not only have a kindly remembrance of the missionaries; in addition, they long to
see them. The Greek word here translated long is a strong
word and has within it the meaning of "yearning after." It
is a present participle, showing constancy. The deep yearning was felt constantly. The Thessalonians long to see the
missionaries who had brought the gospel to them. Thus
Paul joyfully relates what Timothy has reported to him and,
with a comparative clause, he hastens to assure the Thessalonians that this longing is mutual: as we long to see you.

[7] Again Paul addresses his readers with the affectionate brethren. For this reason, he writes, referring to the
favorable report brought by Timothy regarding the faith,
the love, and the kindly remembrance of the Thessalonians.
It is because of this good news that Paul can make the
claims which follow.

In all our distress and affliction is a phrase indicating
one reason the good news brought by Timothy was so
welcome. Distress is a word that denotes pressing anxieties;
it applies especially to physical hardships or outward con-
straints. Paul uses the same word in speaking of "the im-
pending distress" when writing to the Corinthians (1 Cor.
7:26), and when speaking of the "necessity" which had
been placed upon him to preach the gospel (1 Cor. 9:16).
The word thus may be used to describe constraint which a
person feels due to surrounding circumstances or that
which comes from feeling a sense of duty. The word afflic-

71

⁸ for now we live, if you stand fast in the Lord.

tion refers in a special way to crushing troubles which are
heaped upon men by others as in persecutions. Paul used
the same word in 1:6 when describing the "much affliction"
in which the people of Thessalonica had received the gospel (see also 2 Thess. 1:4). Paul and his companions had
been in both **distress** and **affliction.** Paul had come into the
black night of the paganism of Corinth without money and
without friends. He was soon under vicious attack by the
Jews of that city. Figuratively speaking, he was in the very
shadow of death.

Paul describes the effects of Timothy's news: **we have
been comforted.** The verb has within it the ideas both of
comforting and strengthening. It is the same word used in
verse 2, translated "to exhort," concerning one of the purposes for the sending of Timothy to Thessalonica. Further,
Paul says that the comfort they had felt was **about you,**
indicating the basis of the comfort and strength which the
missionaries had derived from Timothy's report (cf. 2 Cor.
7:6ff.). The strength which they feel surging within them is
based on the faith and commitment of Thessalonians, and
Paul wants these people to know that fact. **Through your
faith** is further explanatory of the part played by the Thessalonians in reviving the spirits of Paul and his helpers.
These men in **distress** and **affliction** were comforted,
strengthened, and revived through the **faith** of a group of
people in whom they were intensely interested. Timothy
told Paul and his co-workers about that faith and it is that
faith which strengthens them.

[8] The **for** of verse 8 looks back to the entire preceding
statement of verse 7, the statement that the missionaries
have been comforted because of the good news brought by
Timothy. **Now** seems to have its full temporal force with
the idea being, "now that we have received such good
news." The present tense, **we live,** indicates a continuous
state as if to say, "we continue to live." The idea is that the

⁹ For what thanksgiving can we render to God for you, for
all the joy which we feel for your sake before our God,

---

missionaries again see life having purpose and meaning;
they have been revived to the extent that they feel a new
energy even in the midst of trials. Whereas they had previously felt as if they were walking in the shadow of death,
they now see the sun shining again. They feel a dynamic
power and an inner serenity resulting from Timothy's favorable report.

The condition upon which the missionaries' living is
contingent is: **if you stand fast in the Lord.** The construction could be translated, "since you are standing fast in the
Lord." Timothy has just brought the information to Paul
that the Thessalonians are standing fast. Paul and his helpers **live** since this is true. However, the construction in the
Greek is such that there is an element of futurity in the
statement as well as the present durative idea. Paul suggests that they will continue to see life with all of its fulness
and power if the Thessalonians continue to stand fast in the
Lord (cf. 2 Thess. 2:15). There is an emphatic **you** in the
Greek, impressing upon the Thessalonians the fact that it is
upon their standing fast that life for the missionaries depends. The prepositional phrase, **in the Lord,** denotes the
sphere in which the readers stand and are to continue to
stand. To stand **in the Lord** means to remain steadfastly in
union with Christ by an unshaken faith.

[9] With **for** Paul introduces a confirmation of the preceding conditional statement. "We live," says Paul, and
then, **for what thanksgiving can we render to God for you?**
Paul is expressing in fervent terms his heartfelt thanks for
the Thessalonians and for the joy they have brought to his
heart. The question asked by Paul is rhetorical. It implies
that Paul and his companions feel utterly unable to give
back **to God** in return for the abundance of **joy** which they
feel. Thanksgiving is thought of as a kind of return for the
blessings of God. The word translated **render** is from a

¹⁰ praying earnestly night and day that we may see you face to face and supply what is lacking in your faith?

---

double compound verb signifying to give back in return for. And again, the phrase, **for you,** gives emphasis to the importance of the Thessalonians to the writers.

For all the joy indicates the basis or the ground for the thanksgiving of which the writers speak. And the relative clause, **which we feel for your sake,** defines the joy more accurately. Once again, the expression, **for your sake,** emphasizes the significant role played by the Thessalonians in bringing this joy to the hearts of the writers. These men are rejoicing, their hearts are running over with joy, and they feel inadequate to express their gratitude for it. But the true nature of their rejoicing is suggested by the phrase, **before our God.** It is not that joy which arises from a selfish nature; it is purely unselfish, and they are willing to lay it all before the eyes of their God whom they recognize as the true source of such joy. Even though they make it quite emphatic that it is the Thessalonians who are the basis of their joy, yet they emphasize that after all it is God to whom the thanksgiving must be rendered.

[10] Living in the atmosphere of gratitude and joy, the writers now express their petition to God. The word from which **praying** comes is not the ordinary word used for prayer; it is a stronger word and carries with it a sense of personal need. Though in the midst of great elation, the writers feel personal needs and pray accordingly. The word from which **earnestly** is translated is a double compound adverb, an emphatic way of expressing abundance. Paul is the only New Testament writer who uses the word and he uses it only three times: 3:10, in 5:13 where it is translated "very highly," and in Ephesians 3:20 where it is translated "exceeding abundantly." The word is intensely earnest, conveying the idea of overabundance. The praying of Paul and his helpers was more than the mere saying of prayers.

The praying which the missionaries are doing is described as taking place **night and day.** The expression is adverbial, indicating that the praying was done within the night and within the day. The same expression was used describing the time of the labors of the missionaries (see notes on 2:9). The idea is that of constancy in prayer. The prayers of these men arise from fervor of heart and ascend to God unceasingly.

The purpose of the intense praying being done by Paul and his helpers was that they might **see** the Thessalonians **face to face and supply what is lacking in your faith.** Paul has before told of their desire to see the Thessalonians and also of their efforts to see them (2:17). Here he declares that such a reunion is the purpose for which he and his friends pray. Seeing these Thessalonian Christians again would be a real pleasure to these evangelists. However, as Paul goes ahead to show, it was not merely for the sake of seeing these people that he prayed for a reunion with them. He feels that they can do something to help the church. He realizes that there are yet defects in the **faith** of the Thessalonians. The original word from which **supply** comes is used of material affairs concerning such an activity as "mending" nets (Matt. 4:21); in the spiritual realm it is used to indicate "equipment" for God's people (Eph. 4:12). Paul has something like this in mind, something that would help bring the young Christians to a state of maturity, as he prays to God to grant him a visit to Thessalonica.

The word from which the expression, **what is lacking,** comes means "shortcomings" and is plural, indicating that more than one facet in the lives of the Thessalonians needs to be brought to maturity. Thus both the verb **supply** and the noun which is translated **what is lacking** indicate deficiencies existing among these people. Paul describes these deficiencies as something which they lack in their faith. This does not mean that Paul was disappointed in the Thessalonians. He does not necessarily imply that Timothy has in any way brought an adverse report concerning them.

¹¹ Now may our God and Father himself, and our Lord
Jesus, direct our way to you;

In fact, as he has already indicated, the report brought by
Timothy was of such nature as to bring joy to his heart. But
Paul knows that, though basic doctrinal teaching had been
done among the Thessalonians, certain points need emphasis or clarification and they need to be related to life more
and more. He knows that the Christians in Thessalonica are
human beings; he also knows that the work of the missionaries among them had been limited by lack of time. He is
aware of the fact that, however faithful these people may
have been or however rapidly they may have grown, there
must yet be qualities which need to be brought to maturity.
A glance at the epistle as a whole reveals that Paul desires
the readers to abound "more and more" in virtues which
they had already exhibited (4:1, 10); that he knows their
need for more thorough instruction regarding the second
coming of Christ and the resurrection (4:13ff.); and that he
realizes that there are idle ones, fainthearted ones, and
weak ones within the church (5:14). Surely, all of this is
before his mind as he prays that he and his friends might be
permitted a visit to Thessalonica.

Good Wishes and Prayers, 3:11–13

[11] The writers now pour out their hearts in expressions of prayers and wishes, enlarging upon what they have
said in the preceding verse. They appeal to **our God and
Father** and make the address intensive by using the emphatic **himself.** They realize that, however strong the needs
in Thessalonica may seem, and however strong their desires
to go there may be, they must look to God for leadership
and guidance. Then, **our Lord Jesus** is linked with the
name of **God** and the two have a common verb. This
linking of Jesus with the Father is significant; also significant is the fact that the writers ascribe to Jesus, along with
the Father, a power in directing the affairs of their lives. It

¹² and may the Lord make you increase and abound in love
to one another and to all men, as we do to you,

---

shows that in this early letter of Paul the deity of Jesus was
recognized and proclaimed. In fact, there is no time, however early, when Jesus was not so regarded. All of the
available evidence points to the fact that the deity of Christ
was a fact proclaimed by him and believed by the first
disciples, and that it was not an accretion imposed upon
Jesus and his teachings by a later church.

The verb **direct** expresses a petition—a function of the
Greek optative mood. Quite noticeable in the original is the
fact that the verb is singular even though it has a plural
subject. This gives emphasis to the unity of the Father and
the Son. Paul looks to both in hope that all obstacles which
had previously stood in the way will be removed and that
he and his colleagues will be directed to Thessalonica.

[12] Again using optatives in expressing a prayer, Paul
informs the Thessalonians as to the objects of their prayers
for them. The verbs **increase** and **abound** are practically
synonymous. The latter is the word used most frequently
by Paul and perhaps is a bit stronger than **increase**. The use
of the two seems to be a device for the purpose of emphasis.
The noun which is to be connected with both verbs is **love**.
First, Paul desires that their love **increase and abound**
toward **one another**. He has already made reference to their
"labor of love" (1:3). But he desires that this love among
the brethren for one another grow stronger as, indeed, it
should ever be doing. But their love is not to stop there; it is
to go out to and abound toward **all men** (cf. Matt. 5:43ff.;
Gal. 6:10). The Greek language has other words for love
but the word used here (*agapē*) designates the highest
possible type of love. It is that love which God has for all
men (John 3:16) and which those who are the children of
God should have for all men. It is that love which looks
upon others with consideration and regard, which desires
that which is good for them, and which is willing to give of

¹³ so that he may establish your hearts unblamable in holiness before our God and Father, at the coming of our Lord Jesus Christ with all his saints.

---

self to promote their good. It does not demand that its object be worthy. This kind of love goes out to those who are unworthy. This is the kind of love Paul wants the Thessalonians to have and in which he wants them to abound toward each other and toward all men. The comparative clause, as we do to you, is a reference to the love which Paul and his co-workers have for the Thessalonians. Paul is saying that he wants the love of the Thessalonians to abound just as the love of himself and his friends abounds toward them. He appeals to them to do what he and his helpers are doing, thus strengthening his plea by an appeal to example.

[13] The writers now state the purpose of the Lord's making the Thessalonian Christians to increase and abound in love, that purpose being so that he may establish. . . . The word establish is the same word used in verse 2 concerning the purpose for the sending of Timothy to Thessalonica. The word hearts points to the inward man as that which is to be established or strengthened. Paul believes that an abounding love will establish, make firm, and strengthen the heart. The adjective unblamable describes the condition of heart for which Paul is hoping, and the prepositional phrase, in holiness, indicates that the one who maintains an unblamable heart is to do so as one set apart entirely to the service of God (cf. 2:10).

Paul prays, then, that the hearts of the Thessalonians may be established so that they will be unblamable in holiness; furthermore, this is to be before or "in the sight of" our God and Father (cf. Phil 1:9, 10). Their lives are to be such as can bear the searching eye of God day by day; however, as the phrase at the coming of our Lord Jesus suggests, it is quite evident that the writers specially have in mind the day of judgment when all shall stand before

God. Again, as at the close of chapter 2, the writers look to the coming (*parousia*) of Christ as the consummation of the Christian's hope.

There is some difficulty as to the identity of **all his saints** who will attend the Lord at his **coming.** The word literally means "holy ones" and is the ordinary word for "saints" in the New Testament. On the other hand, Jesus spoke of his coming in these words: "When the Son of man comes in his glory, and all the angels with him . . ." (Matt. 25:31). Paul, in the present passage, speaks of the "saints" or "holy ones" coming with Jesus. Does Paul mean to indicate attendants other than angels? In Mark 8:38 and Luke 9:26, Jesus speaks of the "holy angels." The word in these two passages which is translated "holy" is the same word Paul uses which is translated "saints." Also, the word is used to apply to angels in the Greek Old Testament in such passages as Psalms 89:5; Zechariah 14:5; and others. The Dead Sea Scrolls also furnish examples in which angels are called "holy." And since, as pointed out above, Christ associates angels with his return, it is not unlikely that they are meant here. Also, Paul elsewhere associates angels with the second coming of Christ (2 Thess. 1:7). Morris says that both the departed righteous ones and angels will be associated with Jesus at his coming and that Paul's statement does not necessarily have to be limited to either. It is possible that Paul contemplates the spirits of departed saints who will be associated with Jesus at his coming; or that he contemplates only angels; or that he uses a term which could include both. Whatever may be the precise meaning Paul had in mind, the same general impression of the glorious coming of Jesus Christ is received. He shall appear with a glorious retinue of "all his holy ones."

Paul often closes a section with a prayer or a doxology. He closes this section with a prayer. His prayers reveal his principal concerns. This prayer contains the topics which follow in chapters 4, 5: holiness, brotherly love, and the second coming of Christ.

EXHORTATION AND INSTRUCTION, CHAPTERS 4, 5

In this second major section of the epistle the writers exhort and admonish the Thessalonian Christians in matters of practical Christian living. They also give instruction in matters wherein the Thessalonians are deficient. These admonitions and instructions are by no means haphazard; they are designed to meet the special needs of the community of Christians in Thessalonica. Of some of these needs the writers would be aware because they were universal needs; of others they would be aware because they knew the environment in which the Christians in Thessalonica lived; and of others because, likely, Timothy had reported them upon his return from that city.

There is first the exhortation to continued purity in the midst of heathen temptations with the reminder of what the missionaries had taught while they were in Thessalonica (4:1-8).

Second, there is the exhortation to brotherly love concerning which the Thessalonians had already been taught and which, to a very great degree, they are already practicing (4:9-12).

Next, the writers give certain instructions regarding the second coming of Christ. Evidently some of the members of the church in Thessalonica were concerned about the dead saints and were fearful that these would be at a disadvantage when the Lord returns. The writers assure them that the living saints will not have any advantage over the dead at that day; the dead in Christ shall rise before the living are caught up and all shall together go to meet the Lord (4:13-18).

As to the time of the coming of the Lord, Paul appeals to what the Thessalonians already know: "The day of the Lord will come like a thief in the night." However, he assures Christians that the day will not overtake them as a thief for they are to "keep awake and be sober" (5:1-11).

¹ Finally, brethren, we beseech and exhort you in the Lord
Jesus, that as you learned from us how you ought to live
and to please God, just as you are doing, you do so more
and more.

In the closing verses of the epistle, the writers give
admonitions regarding the attitude of Christians toward
their leaders. They exhort them to maintain peace within
the church. They give exhortations regarding the treatment
of various groups among the Thessalonian Christians. They
admonish the Thessalonians about rejoicing, praying, giving of thanks, and the right attitude toward prophecy
(5:12-22).

Finally, the writers express a prayer for the complete
sanctification of the Thessalonian Christians; they ask for
the prayers of the Thessalonians; they charge that the letter
be read to the entire church; they close with a brief benediction (5:23-28).

Exhortation to Holy Living, 4:1–8

[1] The word which is translated **finally** literally means
"as for the rest." It is a transitional word, sometimes, as here,
introducing ethical exhortations (cf. Eph. 6:10; Phil. 3:1;
4:8; 2 Thess. 3:1). It is at times found toward the end of an
epistle, not signifying the actual conclusion but merely
pointing toward the end (2 Cor. 13:11).

Addressing the readers with the affectionate word,
brethren, the writers employ a twofold injunction: **we beseech and exhort.** The two verbs appear to be practically
synonymous though the second is the stronger of the two.
Doubtless the two are used, with the stronger coming last,
for the sake of emphasis. Paul wants the readers to know
that the exhortation he is giving is an important one. He
also wants them to know that he and his companions are
not urging something upon their own authority; they are
beseeching and exhorting **in the Lord.**

Paul tells his readers that what he is about to exhort

them to do is that which he had taught them to do, evidently referring to the oral teaching of the missionaries while they were in Thessalonica (cf. 2 Thess. 3:6). That which the Thessalonians had learned from the missionaries was: **how you ought to live and to please God.** The infinitive from which **to live** is translated means literally "to walk." Concerning Paul's frequent use of the imagery of walking to describe the Christian life see notes on 2:12. This first infinitive in the exhortation **to live** denotes what the missionaries had taught the Thessalonians to do. The second infinitive phrase, **to please God,** indicates the result of putting into practice that which is enjoined in the first. Paul and his helpers had, while in Thessalonica, taught the Thessalonians how they must **live** and by so doing **to please God.** In 2:4 Paul had said that he and his fellow workers spoke "to please God"; in 2:15 one of the indictments brought against the unbelieving Jews was that they "displease God"; here, to please God, is set forth as a distinctively Christian motive for right living (cf. Rom. 8:8; 1 Cor. 7:32; Gal. 1:10). Paul adds the comparative clause, **just as you are doing.** It may be that he feels that the command might seem to suggest a condemnation of the present conduct of the readers. Paul is ever ready to praise when he feels praise is due. Accordingly, he wants the Thessalonians to know that he has no serious criticism of their present conduct.

Now, having approached the Thessalonians with **we beseech and exhort,** having affirmed that they are doing so **in the Lord,** having reminded them that what they are urging is just what they had taught them previously, and having assured them that they are already doing what they taught, the writers come to the admonition: **you do so more and more.** These are new converts who have made a good beginning but still live in the midst of temptations and do not have full knowledge. The idea is that they are to continue, even to improve, in the practice of living so as to be pleasing to the Lord. Paul is thus urging the Thessaloni-

² For you know what instructions we gave you through the
Lord Jesus. ³ For this is the will of God, your sanctification:
that you abstain from immorality;

---

ans to achieve greater diligence, to make even greater
efforts. Though he has no serious condemnation of them
and, in fact, has much praise for them, still he wishes to
urge upon them the fact that the Christian can never be
satisfied (cf. Paul's prayer for the excellent church at Philippi, Phil. 1:9-11). Paul uses great tact in this exhortation.
He acknowledges the highly successful Christian living of
the readers and yet urges them on to greater heights. His
dealing with them as a nurse with her children or as a
father with his child is still evident (see 2:7, 11).

[2] Again the writers remind the Thessalonians of their
personal ministry among them: **you know what instructions
we gave.** They want them to be assured that they are
continuing to lead them in the way they had previously
taught. Once again they wish to remind the readers that the
commands being given to them are not of their own devis-
ings; so they remind them that the instructions they gave
were **through the Lord Jesus.** Concerning these instructions
and of what they consisted they say to the Thessalonians,
you know.

[3] Advancing to matters of a more specific nature, Paul
says: **for this is the will of God, your sanctification. This** is
the subject of the sentence, **will,** is a predicate nominative,
and **sanctification** is in apposition with **will.** God's will for
the Thessalonians is their **sanctification,** a condition in
which they are wholly set apart for God and separated by
life and conduct from the unbelieving world about them.
Since the primary idea in sanctification is that of being set
apart for God, then, of course, in a very real sense, a person
is sanctified at the time of conversion. Hence, Paul can say
to the Christians at Corinth, "you were sanctified" (1 Cor.
6:11). The state of sanctification is one which the Christian

⁴ that each one of you know how to take a wife for himself
in holiness and honor,

---

must be careful to maintain, as Paul's admonition to the
Thessalonians shows. And, as Paul later indicates in 5:23,
complete sanctification is a goal toward which Christians
may look (cf. Heb. 10:10; 1 Peter 1:15f.). In the passage
now under consideration Paul reminds the Thessalonians
that their **sanctification is the will of God.**

In a series of very meaningful clauses, Paul proceeds to
define sanctification more fully. He first defines it negatively: **that you abstain from immorality.** The word for
immorality refers to illicit sexual acts. There is no indication that there was any specific case of immorality in the
Thessalonian church which Paul was intending to rebuke
as he did when writing to Corinth (1 Cor. 5:1ff.). However,
moral standards were quite low in the Greek cities of the
first century. The word for **immorality** is found in a number
of lists of sins in the New Testament, especially in connection with Gentiles (Acts 15:20, 29; 21:25; 1 Cor. 6:9; 2 Cor.
12:21; Gal. 5:19; Eph. 5:3; Col. 3:5). Converts in these
places came from a background that had a much lower
moral standard than did the Jews of Palestine from whom
the first converts to Christianity came. Paul knows that the
members of the newly-formed church at Thessalonica will
feel the pressures of the world about them; he is aware of
the laxity that prevails among the Gentiles. But he is also
aware of the high standard of morality which is involved in
sanctification to God and is not willing that this be compro-
mised. True consecration is moral as well as religious.

[4] The second item in the definition of sanctification is
on the positive side: **that each one of you know how to take
a wife for himself in holiness and honor.** The word from
which the RSV translates **wife** is *skeuos*. The meaning of
the word is "vessel" and there is no justification for translat-
ing it otherwise. Whether the word has reference to one's
wife or to one's body has been discussed by scholars

through the years; however, this is not a matter for translators to decide. Phillips translates the word "body," but his translation is equally as improper as is that of the RSV.

Many commentators hold that his own vessel has reference to one's wife (e.g., Robertson, Lenski, Frame, Ellicott). Among older commentators, Augustine also held this view. These point out that in rabbinical literature this use of the word is found. Further, they point out that the Greek *ktasthai*, which the RSV translates "to take," primarily means "to acquire," and that one does not acquire one's own body. Thayer points out that the word is used of acquiring or marrying a wife. Paul elsewhere recommends marrying a wife as a means of preventing fornication (1 Cor. 7:2), and Peter speaks of the wife as a vessel (1 Peter 3:7).

Other commentators (e.g., Findlay, Milligan, Morris; and among older commentators Tertullian, Chrysostom, Calvin) take the view that "his own vessel" has reference to one's own body. Some of these (e.g., Milligan and Morris) maintain that "wife" is not the natural meaning which one gets from the passage. Morris points out that 1 Peter 3:7 has no bearing on the question at all since the passage contemplates both husband and wife as vessels and does not consider the wife as the vessel of the husband. Findlay points to 2 Corinthians 4:7 in which Paul affirms that the treasure has been placed in "earthen vessels" and to 2 Corinthians 5:1 in which the body is called an "earthly tent." As to the word, *ktasthai*, Milligan cites instances from the papyri in which it is used to mean "possess." Morris quotes from Moulton and Milligan who refer to a papyrus dated A.D. 23 where the verb means "have." Morris also quotes from *The Epistle of Barnabas* VII, 3 in which the expression "vessel of His Spirit" has reference to the body of Christ. He also cites a passage from Hermas in which *skeuos* refers to the body (*Mandate* V, 1, 2).

It does seem that to take "vessel" as referring to one's body is the more natural view, and it was the view held by most of the early commentators. Several passages speak of persons as vessels (Acts 9:15; Rom. 9:21-23; 2 Cor. 4:7; 2 Tim. 2:21), but in no passage (unless it be the one under consideration) is a wife or husband spoken of as being the vessel of the other. In 1 Peter 3:7 where *skeuos* is used to refer to the wife, she is said to be the "weaker vessel" (ASV); however, she is the weaker of the two in the sense that her body is not as strong as that of the man. Evidently, Peter is thinking of the body which he designates as the "weaker vessel." As pointed out above, *ktasthai* can have the meaning of "have" or "possess." However, even the retention of the primary meaning of the verb, "to acquire," fits in very well with this view since the body is to be mastered or subdued (see 1 Cor. 6:18ff.).

In an Old Testament passage, David said, "The vessels of the young men are holy," and he said this in reply to the priest who wanted to know if "the young men have kept themselves from women" (1 Sam. 21:4, 5). Paul says the Christian is to know how to *ktasthai* his vessel in holiness and honor. The Greek verb "to know" used here is iterative. Knowing how to maintain purity is not a momentary impulse, but a constant process. Possessing one's vessel in holiness and honor is a lesson that must be learned, but it is a necessary part of the process of complete sanctification. The Christian must learn to come into possession of his own body or to bring it into subjection. "I pommel my body and subdue it" is the way Paul described his own battle of self-mastery (1 Cor. 9:27). In another passage the apostle expressed it this way: "For just as you once yielded your members to impurity and to greater and greater iniquity, so now yield your members to righteousness for sanctification" (Rom. 6:19). Regardless of whether *ktasthai* be taken in the sense of acquiring or in the sense of possessing, the passage still makes good sense when *skeuos* is taken to refer to one's body. Ellicott says it is not easy to make discrimination at this point since the ideas of acquiring and possessing were often expressed by the same word. The objection,

⁵ not in the passion of lust like heathen who do not know
God;

---

therefore, to interpreting "vessel" as referring to the body
on the ground that it would necessitate giving to *ktasthai*
an unwarranted meaning is not such a formidable one.

In addition, the tense of **know how to** indicates an
habitual state, not merely a single action. Every person
whom Paul is exhorting is to learn how to do what he here
enjoins. Furthermore, each person whom Paul is exhorting
is urged to possess himself of **his own** vessel, as the Greek
text has it. If Paul is urging men to learn how to acquire a
wife, as the alternative position alleges, then Paul is speaking only to men and to unmarried ones at that. This is not
impossible but does not seem to be the general tenor of the
passage. And it does seem that the "vessel" of which Paul
speaks is already the property of those to whom he addresses the appeal. However, regardless of the view one
adopts as to the identity of "vessel" and the significance of
ktasthai, the main thrust of the passage can still be seen to
be that of purity of life as a necessary part of the process of
sanctification. The prepositional phrase, **in holiness and
honor,** indicates the high realm in which the possessing of
one's vessel is to be wrought.

[5] Another prepositional phrase, **not in the passion of
lust,** brings out negatively the contrast which was introduced by the phrase, **in holiness and honor,** of verse 4. The
state of lustful passion is the very opposite of holiness and
honor. It is descriptive of the one who is mastered by his
lusts. Those who think of *skeuos* as referring to a wife see in
this phrase a description of the wrong way for a man to
enter into marriage; they see in the prepositional phrase of
verse 4 the high ideal of marriage and the idea of holy
union between husband and wife. Those who think of
skeuos as referring to one's body see in the phrase of verse 5
a prohibition of permitting the body to be in a state of
lustful passion, and they see in the phrase of verse 4 the

⁶ that no man transgress, and wrong his brother in this
matter,ᶜ because the Lord is an avenger in all these things,
as we solemnly forewarned you.
    ᶜ Or *defraud his brother in business*

---

idea of using the body in high and honorable service (cf.
Rom. 6:19). The comparative clause introduced by like
makes a comparison between the Gentiles and the group
addressed by Paul as "each of you." The Gentiles know
gods, but they **do not know God** (cf. Ps. 79:6 as illustration
of the Old Testament's description of pagans as those who do
not know God). Paul seems to consider this fact a sufficient
explanation for their state of lustful passion and the fact
that the Thessalonians do know God a sufficient ground for
purity of life. In Romans 1 Paul elaborates more fully upon
the sensual practices of the Gentiles; in the same chapter he
makes it quite clear that their sensual conduct was due to
their wrong ideas about God (cf. 1 Peter 1:13ff.).

[6] Paul continues to define the matter of sanctification,
a subject which he introduced in verse 3. The word **transgress** has the meaning of going beyond certain prescribed
limits or of overreaching; wronging has within it the idea of
depriving others of rights which are theirs. Transgressing or
defrauding a **brother,** or any person for that matter, is a
violation of the standard which sanctification demands. The
Greek text, literally, is "in the matter." This phrase defines
the realm in which the transgressing and the defrauding of
a brother are prohibited.

Some commentators (e.g., Lenski, Moffatt, Hendriksen)
think Paul is making a definite transition from the subject
of sensuality to the subject of honesty and fairness in business matters. Lenski claims that the word, *pragmati,* translated **matter,** was a business term and that a discussion of
commercial matters comes most naturally at this point since
sexual immorality and commercial greed were two of the
outstanding sins of the pagan world. He also points out that
the idea of covetousness is to be found in the word trans-

lated **wrong.** The metaphors of the business world included
in Paul's admonition are pointed out also by Moffatt who
alleges that Paul is not necessarily changing from the subject of immorality but is still dealing with it, only now in
the form of dishonesty and fraud. Thayer cites this passage
as an instance in which *pragmati* is used in a business
sense; however, he gives other definitions of the word and
cites passages in which it has reference to other affairs
(Matt. 18:19; Rom. 16:2).

On the other hand, some commentators (e.g., Robertson, Lightfoot, Ellicott, Findlay, Milligan) think **the matter**
has reference to the sin of immorality which was previously
discussed by Paul. They see verse 6 as a natural continuation of the subject under discussion. They point out that in
fornication there is a wrong against someone other than the
parties immediately involved, that the sin is definitely a
violation of the rights of another. Therefore, they say, the
one who is guilty of such immorality does go beyond
the rights which are his and defraud another. They regard
the entire context as lending support to this view.

To decide whether Paul is beginning a new discussion
relating to business matters or continuing his discussion of
sensuality is not easy. Though dogmatism is not in order at
this point, it does seem that the view which regards this as
a continuation of the discussion of immorality has the
stronger case. Paul's designation of **the matter** seems to
indicate that he expects his readers to continue thinking
along the same line he has been leading them. The use of
the definite article serves to point to the subject under
discussion—**the matter**—rather than to call attention to a
new matter or subject.

With the word **because** Paul passes to a discussion of
reasons for the prohibitions he has given. The first reason
is: **because the Lord is an avenger in all these things.** The
comprehensive expression, **all these things,** includes all the
sins he has mentioned. In calling the Lord **an avenger** Paul
is employing a descriptive term which is familiar to stu-

⁷ For God has not called us for uncleanness, but in holiness.

---

dents of both the Old Testament and the New Testament
(2 Sam. 4:8; 22:48; Deut. 32:43; Lk. 18:7; Rom. 12:19; Rev.
18:20). God is one who gives judgment, avenges, takes
vengeance. The consequences of failure to live in accordance with moral law are inevitable. Paul in Romans 1
discusses the consequences of immorality in this present
life. He likely does not mean to exclude this as he writes to
the Thessalonians; but it is also likely, in view of the
references in the epistle to the second coming of Christ,
that Paul has the final requital uppermost in his thinking.

Once again Paul emphasizes that he is repeating by
letter what he and his colleagues had previously told the
Thessalonians in person: **as we solemnly forewarned you.**
The vengeance of the Lord is not something new to these
Christians. While with them Paul had forewarned or predicted that the Lord would avenge all manner of unchast-
ity. In the Greek text Paul employs two verbs in this sentence. The other might well be translated, "We solemnly
witnessed." Paul employs the word only here and in three
other passages (1 Tim. 5:21; 2 Tim. 2:14; 4:1). It is used in
the sense of solemnly testifying before God. The use of the
word in the present connection reveals the solemn manner
in which Paul had warned the Thessalonians of the coming
wrath of God. The RSV seeks to capture the force of the
second verb in the sentence by using the word **solemnly**
with the other verb.

[7] Paul introduces a second reason for the prohibitions. Having reminded the Thessalonians of the vengeance
the Lord will take upon the disobedient, he adds that God's
call had a moral end in view, that of **holiness.** Paul's reference to God's call would remind the readers of their hearing the gospel and their response to it (cf. 2 Thess. 2:14).
Looking at the matter from a negative viewpoint, God had
not called them with the purpose in view of their living for
uncleanness. Positively, the prepositional phrase, **in holi-**

⁸ Therefore whoever disregards this, disregards not man but God, who gives his Holy Spirit to you.

---

ness, designates the sphere or atmosphere in which God expects those whom he calls to live. The word here translated **holiness** is the exact word which is translated "sanctification" in verse 3. Paul's insistence, then, is that the will of God for the Christian is sanctification. He then proceeds to define sanctification. He now returns to urge that one reason God **called** the Thessalonians was for their sanctification. They should therefore walk in harmony with the purpose for which they were called.

[8] With the word **therefore** Paul now draws a conclusion from the truths upon which he has elaborated. For the Thessalonians to disregard these moral principles would not be a rejection of any **man**. There is a sense in which it would imply a rejection of Paul and his co-laborers, but Paul wants to impress upon them that, in the final analysis, it would be a rejection of **God** who is the author of these laws.

Paul describes God as the one **who gives his Holy Spirit to you.** God gives the Holy Spirit to dwell in a person at the time he becomes a child of God (Acts 2:38; 5:32; Rom. 5:5; 2 Cor. 1:22; Gal. 4:6; 1 John 3:24). In the present passage Paul describes God as the one who continues to give the Holy Spirit to the Christian. **Gives** is from a present participle and this indicates continuous giving. The Holy Spirit continues to dwell in the Christian because God so wills it and bestows the Spirit as a constant gift. The man who breaks God's moral law, therefore, is not rejecting man, nor is he merely sinning against God who once gave the Holy Spirit, but against God who is continually giving his Holy Spirit. Impure living is an impious act of defiance against **God** who gives the Spirit even at the time he is proffering the gift. Paul connects the Holy Spirit with sanctification (1 Cor. 6:11; 2 Thess. 2:13f.; 1 Pet. 1:2). He makes a strong appeal for morality, in his discussion of fornication, upon

⁹ But concerning love of the brethren you have no need to have any one write to you, for you yourselves have been taught by God to love one another;

---

the basis that the Holy Spirit dwells in the Christian (1 Cor. 6:18-20).

Exhortation to Brotherly Love, 4:9–12

[9] After discussing purity of life, the writers turn to other practical matters. Having warned against heathen vices, they now come to speak of the outstanding virtue of the religion of Christ, **love.** Some (e.g., Frame) think that the way this section is introduced—**but concerning**—suggests that the Thessalonians had written Paul asking for information on these particular questions. They call attention to the identical form in 1 Corinthians preceding Paul's answers to questions he had received in a letter from Corinth (e.g., 7:1, 25; 8:1; 12:1; 16:1). If the Thessalonians wrote a letter to Paul, nothing is said about it. Such is possible. However, the formula, **now concerning,** would be just as appropriate in introducing matters pertaining to a question brought orally by Timothy. Or it might even introduce a subject concerning which the Thessalonians had made no inquiry.

Paul goes ahead to assure the Thessalonians that they do not **need to have** anything written regarding **love of the brethren.** The Greek word is *philadelphia,* a word which, in the New Testament, is used to describe love within the brotherhood of believers (Rom. 12:10; Heb. 13:1; 1 Peter 1:22). The reason the Thessalonians do not need any additional written instructions regarding brotherly love is that they **have been taught by God** to have this affection for one another. Again emphasis is given to the divine origin of the teaching they had previously had; it had its origin in **God** and not in the human teachers who brought the teaching to them. Because the missionaries had spoken by the inspira-

[10] and indeed you do love all the brethren throughout
Macedonia. But we exhort you, brethren, to do so more and
more, [11] to aspire to live quietly, to mind your own affairs,
and to work with your hands, as we charged you;

---

tion of the Spirit, the Thessalonians can be said to be
"God-taught."

[10] In addition to having been taught of God to practice brotherly love, the Thessalonians are indeed practicing
that which they have been taught to do. Paul states this fact
in further confirmation of his statement that they do not
need to be taught concerning brotherly love. As a matter of
fact, they are showing forth this great virtue not only in a
local sense but **throughout all Macedonia,** the area of
which Thessalonica was the center. However, though ac-
knowledging the present continuous exercise of brotherly
love among the Thessalonian Christians, Paul affectionately
addresses them again as **brethren** and tenderly exhorts
them **to do so more and more.** This is very similar to the
type of exhortation he gives in verse 1. Paul never wants
Christians to be satisfied with their level of achievement; he
wants them to abound, to grow, to excel.

[11] Paul does not end his exhortation with the admonition that the Thessalonians abound in brotherly love. He
now follows with a series of exhortations regarding matters
which may be regarded as the fruits of brotherly love. First,
with two infinitives he exhorts the readers **to aspire to live
quietly.** A calm spirit, an inner tranquillity, is that for
which Paul is urging the Thessalonians to strive. This is the
opposite of an anxious, troubled, disturbed state of mind
(cf. Matt. 6:25ff.; John 14:1; Phil. 4:6f.). In the next infinitive clause of the exhortation, Paul urges each Christian to
focus his attention where it belongs: **to mind your own
affairs.** A restless, troubled spirit has the tendency to cause
one to intrude into the affairs of others. Love for one's
brethren does not produce an inner restlessness nor a desire

¹² so that you may command the respect of outsiders, and
be dependent on nobody. ¹³ But we would not have you
ignorant, brethren, concerning those who are asleep, that
you may grieve as others do who have no hope.

---

to manage the affairs of other people. Further, with another
infinitive Paul admonishes: **work with your hands.** A restless spirit and a desire to intrude into the affairs of others
would naturally cause one to neglect his own duties. Paul
gives dignity to manual labor and insists that honest toil to
support self and family is a part of Christianity (cf. 2
Thess. 3:6-12; Eph. 4:28; 1 Tim. 5:8). Once again, Paul
calls attention to the fact that what he is here enjoining is
nothing new but is **as we charged you.** He and his colleagues had exhorted the Thessalonians in this same vein
while living among them.

[12] Having delineated the various items included in
his exhortation, Paul expresses, in two clauses, the purpose
of his exhortation. First, **that you may command the respect
of outsiders,** suggests that the Thessalonian Christians, by
abounding in brotherly love, by maintaining a calm spirit,
by giving attention to their own affairs, and by working
with their own hands, will win the respect of their unbelieving neighbors. With Paul, this is important (cf. Col.
4:5). Conduct opposite to that which Paul has described
will bring discredit upon the religion which he so earnestly
seeks to promote. The second clause explaining the purpose
of the exhortation is: **and be dependent on nobody.** By
giving heed to the various admonitions contained in the
exhortation the Thessalonians will be able to lead respect-
able lives in the community and will be independent citizens rather than parasites.

Instructions Regarding the Second Coming, 4:13-18

[13] The writers now move to a discussion of an entirely different matter—the dead in Christ. There was evi-

dently, among some of the members of the church in Thessalonica, an anxiety over matters pertaining to the coming of the Lord; the matter over which they were especially disturbed related to the part the dead saints would have in the blessings connected with the second coming of Christ. There seems to have been a fear that the dead saints would not enjoy the same blessings as would be enjoyed by those who would be alive at the time of the second coming. There is no indication of the manner in which this question came to have such prominence. It could be that the death of some of the church members caused the attention of those remaining to be directed to the question. Nor is there any indication of how Paul came to know of their troubled state of mind. A letter from the Thessalonians requesting such information as Paul here gives is within the realm of possibility. It is also likely that Timothy conveyed to Paul something of the state of mind of the Thessalonians and their need for more information regarding these matters.

The clause with which Paul begins the discussion is negative in form but it has a positive meaning: **we would not have you ignorant, brethren.** This is one of Paul's emphatic expressions and is used by him especially when he is referring to personal matters, or correcting erroneous ideas, or giving information on difficult and bothersome questions (cf. Rom. 1:13; 11:25; 1 Cor. 10:1; 12:1; 2 Cor. 1:8; for a similar expression, see 1 Cor. 11:3; Col. 2:1; Phil. 1:12). It is a way Paul has of saying he does not want his readers to be uninformed. It would have been impossible for Paul and his fellow workers to have instructed the Thessalonians completely in all important matters during the short time they had been in their midst. They had evidently done some teaching regarding the second coming of Christ. However, there were some points the Thessalonians did not yet understand. They also need to understand better how to make practical application to the Christian life of the matters they had already learned. It was this deficiency which Paul is seeking to supply in the present letter.

The specific matter concerning which the writers want the Thessalonians to be better informed has to do with **those who are asleep.** Paul elsewhere spoke of death as a sleep (1 Cor. 15:51); Jesus also employed the figure (Matt. 9:24). However, the depicting of death as a sleep is not limited to biblical writers. It has been done on a very widespread scale, even by those whose view of death is totally different from that of the Christian. Findlay suggests that, in the biblical use of the figure, sleep suggests something of the temporary nature of death as well as the idea of rest for the child of God.

Paul next states the purpose for what he has said in the entire preceding statement of the verse: **that you may not grieve as others do who have no hope.** He wants the Thessalonians to be informed concerning those who sleep in order that they will **not grieve as others** grieve. The present tense of **grieve** indicates that the Thessalonians are not to continue grieving. Paul is not forbidding grief of any sort; it is natural for one to grieve who has lost a relative in death. A Christian may experience a personal grief in such a loss and he may weep over his own loss. But he will not weep for those in Christ who have passed on if he understands their true condition. He may rejoice for them while he weeps over his own loss. However, he is not to grieve as others do. The comparative clause **as others do who have no hope** gives emphasis to this thought. The **hope** of which Paul here speaks and which he believes will mitigate grief is that distinctly Christian hope which is grounded in Jesus. The Greeks had a concept of continued existence in another life, but the content of their hope was vastly different from the content of the Christian hope upon which Paul elaborates in the entire passage (vss. 13-18). Too, the Christian hope is different in that it is rooted in an historical person and upon what he has done and promised. The Christian's hope is his confidence in what God will do (cf. Rom. 8:18-25); it is based upon what he has already done. These distinct elements of the Christian's hope are missing from

¹⁴ For since we believe that Jesus died and rose again, even so, through Jesus, God will bring with him those who have fallen asleep.

---

other religions. In Paul's day, the unbelieving world was characterized by a hopeless and bleak despair in the presence of death. Their idea of continued existence after death amounted to hopelessness in Paul's way of thinking; they had "no hope" and were "without God" (Eph. 2:12).

[14] With **for** Paul gives the reason for saying the Thessalonian Christians should not continue to grieve for those who are asleep as others who are without hope grieve. He says **since we believe that Jesus died and rose again,** thus showing that he knows the Thessalonians share belief in these great facts along with the writers. This gives a remarkable insight into the substance of the preaching which Paul and his helpers had done in Thessalonica—facts which the Thessalonians had welcomed and acknowledged as truth (cf. 1 Cor. 15:3-5, 12ff.). The resurrection of Christ occupied a vital place in both the preaching and the writing of inspired preachers (Rom. 4:24; 10:9; 14:9). The doctrine of the resurrection seems to have been a particularly difficult doctrine for the Greeks. When Paul preached the resurrection at Athens, "some mocked" (Acts 17:32). There is quite a similarity between Paul's discussion of the resurrection in 1 Corinthians 15 and his discussion here in 1 Thessalonians. Both were written to churches which were predominantly Greek.

After saying **since we believe that Jesus died and rose again,** Paul does not go ahead, as might be expected, and say "even so we believe," and then give the substance of what is believed as a consequence. Instead, he makes the direct assertion that **even so, through Jesus, God will bring with him those who have fallen asleep.** In other words, he is declaring that since the great facts of Christ's death and resurrection are believed, then the resurrection of the dead in Christ is a fact to be accepted (cf. 1 Cor. 15:12ff.; 2 Cor.

¹⁵ **For this we declare to you by the word of the Lord, that we who are alive, who are left unto the coming of the Lord, shall not precede those who have fallen asleep.**

4:14). God will bring those who have fallen asleep into the eternal state of glory. What God does for these saints will be **through Jesus,** or through his agency. Moreover, he will bring them **with him,** with Christ, into the state of glory. God will gather his saints through the agency of Jesus to be with Jesus. The use of the name "Jesus" is somewhat unusual in such a context as this. Perhaps Paul wishes to emphasize the identity of the historical person, **Jesus,** with the one who is coming to raise the dead and be with them in glory (cf. Col. 3:4).

[15] The writers proceed to explain the point made in the preceding verse. However, they say by way of confirmation: **For this we declare to you by the word of the Lord.** In appealing to the authority of **the Lord** they show that they wish to impress upon the Thessalonians the fact that what they say is not based upon their own authority but on the teaching of Jesus. Some (e.g., Frame) maintain that Paul here makes reference to some statement Jesus had made during his personal ministry. This view is plausible. It could be that Paul is making a summary statement of the teachings relative to the second coming—teachings which are recorded in the Gospels (e.g., cf. Matt. 24:36ff.; 25:31ff.). However, with this view, it would not be necessary to find every item in the Gospels since Jesus did many things which are not recorded (John 20:30; 21:25), and it is known that he said things which are not recorded in the four Gospels (Acts 20:35). Moreover, Paul often received special revelations (cf. 1 Cor. 11:23; Gal. 1:12; 2:1). The more natural meaning of **the word of the Lord** by which he here speaks is that which sees in it a reference to a revelation which Paul received in a special way (this is the view held by Ellicott, Lightfoot, Milligan, Findlay, and others).

This which the writers declare by the authority of Christ is elaborated upon more fully. The substance of the declaration is that those who shall be living at the time of the Lord's return will have no advantage over those who are dead. They will **not precede** them. Those who are living at that time are described as **we who are alive, who are left until the coming of the Lord.** The use of the plural **we is** taken by Bailey, Frame, and others to point to the conclusion that Paul believed he would be among the living at the time of the Lord's return. It is pointed out by them that the two participles which are in apposition with **we,** translated **who are alive and who are left,** are present participles and indicate that the actions are contemplated as continuing to the time of the Lord's coming.

Others (as Ellicott, Lightfoot, Findlay, Morris) maintain that the conclusion is unwarranted that Paul's use of **we** indicates a feeling of certainty that he would be living at the time of the second coming of Christ. They point out that in other passages Paul also includes himself among those who will be raised from among the dead (1 Cor. 6:14; 2 Cor. 4:14). They further point out that Paul's language certainly implies the possibility that Christ might come within his lifetime but that his statements in other passages imply that he realized the possibility of his being among the dead at that time. In brief, since Paul did not know the time of the Lord's advent, he could not speak with certainty as to his own state at that time. In fact, as Lightfoot, points out, Paul himself declares that the time is uncertain (5:1-2).

Though the writers, in the passage under consideration, use the first person plural in referring to those who would be living at the time of the return of Christ, it is not necessary to conclude from this that they are definitely teaching that they will be alive at that time. Nor is it necessary to conclude from passages in which Paul includes himself among those who will be raised that he definitely believed he would be among the dead at that time. It is

¹⁶ For the Lord himself will descend from heaven with a cry of command, with the archangel's call, and with the sound of the trumpet of God. And the dead in Christ will rise first;

---

merely a way he has of identifying himself with his readers. A modern writer could use both expressions, even within the same work, without being accused of inconsistency or of claiming to know in what state the final day would find him. All Christians should look for the day of the Lord's coming; and writers or speakers, when exhorting others relative to that day, might well place themselves in either category—among those who will be alive or among those who will be dead.

Paul assures the Thessalonians that those who are alive at the time of the Lord's coming **shall not precede those who have fallen asleep.** The particular point over which the Thessalonians are disturbed now becomes evident—it related to the part the dead saints would have in the blessings of the second coming of Christ. In some way Paul has been made aware of the matter concerning which the Thessalonians need further instruction. He knows that they need more assurance regarding their departed friends and loved ones. Hence, he assures them that the living will have no advantage over the dead.

[16] Paul now proceeds to give his reason for affirming that the living will have no advantage over the dead at the time of the Lord's return. He assures the Thessalonians that **the Lord himself will descend from heaven.** The word **himself** gives emphasis to the fact that the Lord in person will descend—not an angel nor some other subordinate (cf. 1:10; 2 Thess. 1:7).

Paul employs three prepositional phrases in describing the descent of the Lord from heaven. The first, **with a cry of command,** denotes an attendant circumstance. The word which is used indicates the shout of a general, used to give orders to soldiers, or the shout of a captain in giving orders to his crew. The idea is more fully defined by the two following phrases. The fact that these two phrases are joined together by **and** indicates that they are in some way explanatory of the first phrase, **with a cry of command.** As Findlay points out, the **cry of command** could either be given by the Lord himself or by means of the voice of someone else or it could be given by means of a trumpet call. Evidently, the thought in the mind of Paul is that the **cry of command** will be given through an archangel (cf. Dan. 10:15ff.; Jude 9). Furthermore, as the third prepositional phrase indicates, the cry of command will be by means of a **trumpet** (cf. 1 Cor. 15:52). The trumpet sound was one of the elements connected with the theophany at Sinai (Ex. 19:16ff.; Heb. 12:19; cf. also Matt. 24:31 for Jesus' use of the trumpet in his apocalyptic discourse). It should be kept in mind, however, that these various details which are given to describe the descending Lord are not necessarily to be taken in a literal sense. They are evidently figures of speech—such figures as would appropriately be connected with the idea of awaking those who sleep. However, the idea here presented—that the cry of command which will be heard when the Lord descends will be given through an archangel and by means of the trumpet of God —is a most impressive one and appropriately leads to the next important point.

The consequence of the word of command is described in these words: **And the dead in Christ will rise first.** It is interesting to note that Paul describes the **dead** saints as being **in Christ** and thus employs the same prepositional phrase that he so often uses to designate the locative of sphere of the living saints. It is these saints who have died about whom the Thessalonians are disturbed. Paul assures the Thessalonians that these saints shall rise at the time of the coming of the Lord. In simple words Paul conveys this great promise (cf. 1 Cor. 15:20-23; Phil. 3:20f.). Paul says nothing about the resurrection of those who are not in Christ; he mentions only those about whom the Thessaloni-

¹⁷ then we who are alive, who are left, shall be caught up
together with them in the clouds to meet the Lord in the
air; and so we shall always be with the Lord.

---

ans were troubled. Paul himself elsewhere taught that there
is to be a general resurrection of the just and unjust, one
resurrection which will include all the dead (Acts 24:15).
Jesus taught that "the hour is coming when all who are in
the tombs will hear his voice and come forth, those who
have done good, to the resurrection of life, and those who
have done evil, to the resurrection of judgment" (John 5:28,
29). Jesus and the New Testament writers taught that there
is to be one resurrection, a resurrection of the just and
unjust. However, Paul does not consider the resurrection of
the unjust as he writes to the Thessalonians. His statement
that **the dead in Christ shall rise first** has been taken by
some to mean that **the dead in Christ** will rise before the
rest of the dead are raised. But the rest of the dead are not
in Paul's mind at all in the present passage. The significance of the word **first** can be seen only when the two
events contemplated by Paul are kept clearly in mind.
These two events are the meeting of the Lord by the living
saints and the resurrection of the dead saints. The living
saints shall by no means precede the dead saints; the dead
saints **shall rise first,** that is, before the living saints go up **to
meet the Lord.** This is brought out more fully in the following verse.

[17] Having assured the Thessalonians that the dead
saints shall rise first, Paul proceeds to introduce the next
event that will take place at the time of the coming of
Christ—the ascension of the living saints **to meet the Lord.**
Paul says this will occur **then,** that is, after the dead are
raised. The expression, **we who are alive, who are left,** is
from the same two participles which are found in verse 15.
Those saints who are living at the time of the Lord's coming
shall be caught up . . . to meet the Lord in the air. But
they shall have **no** precedence over those saints who are

¹⁸ Therefore comfort one another with these words. ¹ But as to the times and the seasons, brethren, you have no need to have anything written to you.

---

dead, for they, having been raised, will accompany them as they are caught up. Those who are alive at the time of the Lord's return shall be caught up together with them. Thus the saints who are living at that time and the dead who have been raised will simultaneously go together to meet the Lord. The translation of Jesus to the eternal sphere was made visible to his disciples by his going upward from them and by his being taken out of sight by a cloud (Acts 1:9). So here, in similar language, Paul describes the removal of God's people from this earthly sphere to the eternal. They go to be with Christ and so we shall always be with the Lord. This is the ultimate bliss for which the Christian hopes (cf. John 14:3; 17:24).

[18] Paul began his discussion of the great events which will take place at the time of the Lord's coming by declaring that he was informing the Thessalonians of these matters to prevent their grieving as those grieve who have no hope. As he concludes, his injunction to comfort one another with these words is very much in order. The Thessalonians are to comfort one another with the words which Paul has written regarding the events which will transpire when the Lord returns. Rather than grieving over the dead as those grieve who have not God, they are to comfort and encourage one another. Paul believes these words which he is writing will be sufficient answer to the troubled state of mind which exists in the Thessalonian church. He therefore urges these Christians to take these words and use them in reciprocal comfort (cf. Heb. 3:13; 10:25).

Regarding the Second Coming, 5:1–11

[1] Having urged the Thessalonians to comfort one another, Paul now goes ahead to exhort them in matters

103

² For you yourselves know well that the day of the Lord will come like a thief in the night.

---

pertaining to the Christian life. He is desirous that they be able to comfort one another regarding the dead in Christ; but he is is also desirous that they conduct themselves in such a way that they will be ready for the Lord's coming. He has discussed the content of the hope in Christ; he now proceeds to a discussion of the consequences of hope in Christ for practical Christian living. In order to proceed with the instructions he wishes to give, Paul introduces a new subject: **the times and the seasons**—new, and yet closely related to the subject discussed in 4:13-18.

The word translated **times** has primary reference to indefinite and extended periods of time; the word translated **seasons** has reference to a definite and particular span of time (cf. Neh. 10:34; 13:31; Dan. 2:21). The first seems to indicate time as such, while the second seems to denote periods of time which are distinguished by certain occurrences within them. The chronological idea is in the first; the qualitative idea is in the second. The expression may have its origin in such passages as Daniel 2:21; 4:23; 7:12. The expression seems to be somewhat of a technical one used in an apocalyptic sense. Jesus himself used the same words used by Paul in answering a question put to him by the disciples concerning the kingdom. He said, "It is not for you to know times or seasons which the Father has fixed by his own authority" (Acts 1:7). Some matters pertaining to the **times and seasons** God has revealed; some he has not. Those which he has revealed Christians need to know. Paul employs almost the same formula, **you have no need . . . ,** that he used in 4:9 regarding brotherly love.

[2] With the explanatory **for** Paul proceeds to explain why it is not necessary for him to write concerning the times and the seasons. It is not that they have any special knowledge of God's timetable but rather that they **know**

well that the day of the Lord will come like a thief in the night. Paul does not state how the Thessalonians came to possess this knowledge; however, his certainty that they have this knowledge and that their knowledge is accurate indicates that he and his helpers had taught the Thessalonians regarding these matters while in their midst. They already know as much about **times and seasons** as any person can know.

The substance of what the Thessalonians know well is that the day of the Lord will come like a thief in the night. In the Greek there is no definite article before either **day or Lord.** This indicates that the expression had come to be somewhat stereotyped—used somewhat as a proper noun. It was an expression used by Old Testament prophets to designate a day in which God would, in some way, bring judgment upon men and nations (e.g., Amos 5:18, 20). The coming day of judgment is one of the great themes of the New Testament, being designated by various expressions such as "the day of the Lord Jesus" (1 Cor. 5:5); "the day of God" (2 Peter 3:12); "the last day" (John 6:39f.); "the great day" (Jude 6) and others. It has reference to the day of the second coming of Christ (see also 2 Thess. 2:2).

Paul speaks with certainty as to the fact of the coming of Christ and he is certain that the Thessalonians know this fact. But there is an element of uncertainty connected with that day as is brought out by the comparative clause, **like a thief in the night.** A thief does not notify a home just precisely when to expect him. Rather, his coming is at a time when he is totally unexpected. The illustration carries with it the idea of the sudden and unexpected coming of the Lord. Jesus used a similar illustration in teaching the unexpected nature of his return (Matt. 24:43); so also did the apostle Peter (2 Peter 3:10). Jesus also emphasized that no man can know the day and the hour of that event (Matt. 24:36; Mk. 13:32; cf. Rev. 16:15). So, as Paul writes to the Thessalonians, he stresses the certainty of the coming of Christ and yet the uncertainty as to the time of it—two

³ When people say, "There is peace and security," then
sudden destruction will come upon them as travail comes
upon a woman with child, and there will be no escape.
⁴ But you are not in darkness, brethren, for that day to
surprise you like a thief.

---

ideas which are found in a number of places in the New
Testament.

[3] Paul proceeds to describe the behavior of unbelievers at the time of the Lord's coming and the effect that
event will have upon them. The day will come at a time
when they are saying, **There is peace and security.** This is
reminiscent of the false prophets of the Old Testament who
proclaimed peace in the face of certain doom (Jer. 6:14;
Ezek. 13:10). Such prophets give to their hearers a feeling
of security but it is a false security; they tell them that all is
well and peaceful even when destruction is near. The apostle Peter reminded Christians of his day that there were
false prophets in former days "just as there will be false
prophets among you . . . bringing upon themselves swift
destruction" (2 Peter 2:1). Paul, in the present passage,
tells his readers that those who have a feeling of security
and who speak words of self-assurance will be interrupted
by **sudden destruction** from which **there will be no escape.**
The word **destruction** does not mean cessation of existence
but complete ruin which comes as a result of banishment
from the presence of the Lord as Paul's use of the word
elsewhere clearly shows (cf. 2 Thess. 1:9). The comparison,
as travail comes upon a woman with child, emphasizes the
fact that the destruction will be swift and sudden. The inevitable nature of the destruction is stated in the vivid declaration, **and there will be no escape.** Paul's teaching in
this passage closely parallels the teaching of Jesus in Matthew 24:36-39, 42-44.

[4] Paul now turns to contrast the Christians in Thessalonica with the unbelievers of the preceding verse. **Darkness** designates the realm or atmosphere of wickedness in

⁵ **For you are all sons of light and sons of the day; we are not of the night or of darkness.**

---

which those live who do not know God. Paul elsewhere designates this realm as "the power of darkness" and teaches that it is the antithesis to the kingdom of Christ (Col. 1:13). Peter also makes use of the metaphor, declaring that God's people have been called "out of darkness into his marvelous light" (1 Peter 2:9). In fact, the use of darkness or of night to describe the realm of evil is somewhat common in the New Testament. Old Testament prophets described the coming day of the Lord as "a day of darkness and gloom" (Joel 2:2; Zeph. 1:15). They associated judgment with darkness.

For that day to surprise you like a thief states the result or consequence of not being **in darkness.** The Greek has "the day" (cf. Mal. 3:19; 2 Cor. 1:14; Phil. 1:10; 2 Thess. 2:2). Clearly the reference is to the day of the Lord's coming. The word here translated **surprise** is translated "seize" in Mark 9:18 and "overtake" in John 12:35. The idea is that of catching or overtaking in an unfriendly or hostile sense. Since unbelievers live **in darkness,** they will be unprepared when the day of the Lord comes. They will be overtaken by that day as by a thief. However, Christians, living in the light, will not thus be overtaken for they will be constantly prepared and watchful. This is both the Christian's hope and concern.

[5] Paul now proceeds to explain further why the day of the Lord will not surprise or overtake the Thessalonian Christians. He confirms his negative statement of verse 4 with a positive declaration: **For you are all sons of light and sons of day.** Just as darkness is a common word in the New Testament descriptive of the realm of evil, so **light** is a common word descriptive of that realm which is the opposite of evil (cf. Acts 26:18; Rom. 13:12; 2 Cor. 6:14; Eph. 5:8f.; 1 Peter 2:9; 1 John 1:7). The expression "son of" is Semitic. Paul speaks of Christians as sons of light. This

implies more than the fact that they are living in a pathway with light shining about them. It suggests, in Semitic thought, kinship with light, belonging to it, characterized by it (cf. Luke 16:8). Some see in Paul's words, **and sons of the day,** an additional thought—a reference to the day of the Lord and the idea that Christians are sons of that day. However, **sons of light and sons of the day** appear to have the same meaning in the sentence and it seems more natural to consider the expression as a double statement for the sake of emphasis.

A double negative follows the double positive: **we are not of the night or of darkness.** It appears that here also Paul is using the two for the sake of emphasis rather than intending a distinction. To say that one is **of the night or of darkness** would imply that he belongs to the realm thus described, that he is characterized by it, that he has a kinship with that realm. But Paul assures the Thessalonians that they **are not of** that realm. However, a change of construction is noticeable in the latter part of the verse. **You are,** the writers had said in the negative declaration; now, in the positive declaration, a transition is made to **we are.** By saying **you are all** the writers are likely intending to assure the Thessalonian church that they regard all the members, even those whom they feel compelled to rebuke, as being of light and of the day. This assurance would be encouraging, especially to the faint-hearted. It is also likely that the writers include themselves along with the Thessalonians in the negative statement as a means of encouragement. The change from "you" to "we" on the part of the writers also indicates great tact for they are getting ready to do some teaching on matters of practical Christian living, and they do not wish to do this as a group standing aloof from the readers and making demands of them; rather they wish to include themselves in the brotherhood of the Thessalonians and as standing in need of these teachings also. They want it to be clearly seen that they include themselves in the exhortations. They show that they recognize

⁶ So then let us not sleep, as others do, but let us keep
awake and be sober.

---

their own need for constancy and growth as well as the
need of the Thessalonians.

[6] **So then,** says Paul, looking back over his previous
statements regarding being of the day and not of the night,
let us not sleep as others do. The word translated **others** is
the same word found in 4:13 where "others" are designated
as those "who have no hope." Paul is here referring to the
same class. They repose in the area of darkness, insensitive
to spiritual values, and with a feeling of security. **Sleep** is
an appropriate figure to describe the attitude and conduct
of such as these. Paul's exhortation to his fellow Christians
at Thessalonica is a plea for them to refrain from such
sleep. He realizes the danger faced by Christians of drifting
back into the carelessness and indifference which had formerly characterized them.

The writers continue their exhortation with the adversative appeal, **but let us keep awake and be sober.** There are
two ideas in this appeal both of which are antitheses to
sleep. First, there is the appeal to **keep awake.** The older
versions translated the verb by the English word "watch,"
and the RSV renders the word in this way in some passages.
When Jesus told his disciples that no man knows the time
of his second coming, he used the word in urging them to
be watchful (Matt. 24:42; 25:13; Mark 13:35). The verb
has within it the idea of determined wakefulness—the idea
of staying awake in order to watch. Christians must never
at any time permit themselves to be lulled into a state of
indifference. They must never drift into sin. To continue
the figure, they must never go to sleep. The second appeal
is **let us be sober.** Sobriety, as here used, indicates a calm
spirit and a life of self-control. The writers use the present
tense in all the verbs of this appeal, indicating that the
conduct for which they plead is to be continuing and
enduring.

⁷ For those who sleep sleep at night, and those who get
drunk are drunk at night. ⁸ But, since we belong to the day,
let us be sober, and put on the breastplate of faith and love,
and for a helmet the hope of salvation.

---

[7] The writers make their exhortation quite vivid by an
illustration concerning activities of the night. Sleeping is an
activity which is associated with the night and is ordinarily
done at night; drunkenness, too, is more often associated
with the night. The facts which the writers state are quite
literal but their significance is not exhausted in the literal.
In the context darkness and light have a spiritual significance and the idea seems to be that the spiritual condition
of those who walk in spiritual darkness is closely akin to the
condition which is ordinarily found in people in the time of
night. It is to be expected that those in darkness should
sleep, be insensitive to spiritual values, for sleep is an
activity which is appropriate to the night. Drunkenness
adds to insensitivity. It is therefore to be expected that
those who live lives devoid of sobriety, who are drunken
and stupefied by sin, should thus be without feeling, for
literal drunkenness is most often associated with literal
darkness. The writers evidently expect their readers to
make this spiritual application of the literal facts they
state.

[8] Paul repeats the exhortation, let us be sober. This is
the same admonition found in verse 6 and has the same
meaning as there—an appeal to a calm life of self-control.
Moreover, the writers appeal for sober living since we
belong to the day. In other words, since Christians belong
to light, they are to live in a way that harmonizes with
light, even as those who live in darkness live in a way that
harmonizes with darkness.

Paul now begins to think of the Christian as a soldier. It
may be that the idea of being awake and vigilant suggested
the metaphor. Romans 13:12 provides a similar context and

⁹ For God has not destined us for wrath, but to obtain
salvation through our Lord Jesus Christ,

---

a similar transition to putting on "the armor of light." Paul
employed the metaphor at various times in his writings (2
Cor. 6:7; 10:4; Eph. 6:11-17). He does not employ a particular item of a soldier's armor to represent the same characteristic of the Christian in each case. For instance, in the
Ephesians passage the **breastplate** is said to be "of righteousness," while here it is said to be **of faith and love.**
Faith, in the Ephesians passage, is the shield. Other varia-
tions among the various passages may be noted. This does
not suggest any sort of contradiction; it merely shows Paul's
variation of details in illustrations. It is not at all unusual to
find a figure of speech used in more than one passage with
a different significance in each passage. Paul does not go
into great detail here as he does in Ephesians 6. He mentions only the two items of **breastplate** and **helmet** (cf. Isa.
59:17). These are the two most important defensive items
and Paul seems to be thinking chiefly of defense against
being overtaken by the coming of the Lord. In Ephesians
he makes mention of an offensive weapon since there he is
thinking of battle against Satan and his emissaries. The
Christian is to defend himself against being unprepared so
that the day of the Lord will not come upon him as a thief.
And within the compass of these two very important defensive items Paul brings the triad of **faith, love, and hope** (as
in 1:3)—virtues which are so important to the defense of
the child of God. **Salvation** specifies the goal of hope; the
Christian hopes for salvation. Here is another instance of
the emphasis in the epistle on events associated with the
second coming of Christ.

[9] The Greek word which is translated **for** in verse 9
literally means "because" and with this introductory word
Paul goes ahead to give the reason for his statement of
verse 8—that reason being God's intention in regard to his
people. Christians are to be sober, putting on the Christian

¹⁰ **who died for us so that whether we wake or sleep we might live with him.**

---

armor, because **God has not destined us for wrath, but to obtain salvation through our Lord Jesus Christ.** God's purpose in taking the initiative and calling men into his kingdom is first stated negatively: **God has not destined us for wrath.** Most likely, **wrath** (as in 1:10) has reference to condemnation at the time of the Lord's coming. This was not God's intention when he called these people to be his people. Further, God's purpose in calling men is stated positively: **but to obtain salvation** (cf. 2 Thess. 2:13). Though there is a sense in which Christians have been saved (cf. Eph. 2:8), there is a sense in which salvation is yet future (cf. Rom. 5:9f.; Phil. 3:20f.; Titus 2:13). It is that future salvation which shall be received at the time of the Lord's return to which Paul makes reference. Salvation is that which God intended that man obtain. However, man obtains salvation, not through human merit, but **through our Lord Jesus Christ. Salvation** is possible because of what Jesus has done for man. However, to say that any human effort is precluded would be to make all of Paul's exhortations meaningless. But there is nothing man can do to merit salvation; in all of his efforts to obtain salvation he must look to Christ as Savior and to the work of Christ as the ground of his salvation.

[10] The work of Christ which is viewed as the cause or the ground of man's salvation is more explicitly stated in verse 10. The fact of his death **for us** is plainly declared. This was the central fact in apostolic preaching and Paul had taught "that it was necessary for the Christ to suffer" during his ministry in Thessalonica (Acts 17:3). He here restates the great fact of the vicarious death of Christ (cf. Rom. 5:10; 1 Cor. 15:3; Col. 1:21f.; Titus 2:14). Paul next proceeds to state the purpose of the death of Christ in these words: **so that whether we wake or sleep we might live with him** (cf. 4:14, 17, 18). To make possible eternal life for

¹¹ Therefore encourage one another and build one another up, just as you are doing. ¹² But we beseech you, brethren, to respect those who labor among you and are over you in the Lord and admonish you,

---

man was the purpose Christ had in view when he died. This life will be with him, an endless fellowship with Jesus Christ. And this life will be ours with him, whether we wake or sleep; that is, if we are among the living (awake) when he comes, we shall live with him, or if we are among the dead (asleep) when he comes, we shall live with him. This is parallel to 4:13-17 (see also Rom. 14:8f.).

[11] **Therefore** of verse 11 indicates that the exhortation which follows is given in view of the foregoing declaration. The exhortation is very similar to that of 4:18. Christians have a mutual responsibility to each other. The Christians at Thessalonica can **encourage one another,** as can all other Christians, with the great truths Paul is setting forth in this epistle. The hope which he sets forth and the promises of which he assures them, to be fulfilled at the time of the Lord's coming, can be used as a matter of mutual encouragement. Too, these promises, together with the admonitions found alongside them, can be used as a means for building **one another up** (cf. Rom. 15:2). Paul, by his writings, intends to do more than comfort Christians. He intends to **build them up** and bring them to a greater level of maturity. He recognizes that the Thessalonians are already doing this as he acknowledges in the comparative clause, **just as you are doing.** He also employs the present tense in the two imperatives, showing that he is telling them to continue to do what he knows they are already doing.

A Series of Practical Admonitions, 5:12–22

[12] Addressing his readers with the affectionate **brethren,** Paul makes a transition to a series of practical admonitions. These exhortations are concerned with the relation-

113

ships among members of the church. First, he asks that they **respect** their leaders. Three participles are used in the Greek to describe these leaders. They are described as **those who labor among you.** The word **labor** is the same word used in 1:3 to designate the "labor of love" of the Thessalonians. It indicates laborious toil. These leaders were working hard and unselfishly for the good of the church. Next, they are described as **over you in the Lord.** The word which the RSV translates "are over" suggests to some an official authority such as that exercised by elders. While the lexicons do give "rule," "direct," etc., as some of its meanings, they also give other meanings. For instance, they say the word sometimes means "to be a protector, or guardian; to give aid" (Thayer); "to be concerned about, care for, give aid" (Arndt-Gingrich). The RSV translates the word in this latter sense in Romans 12:8, "he who gives aid." In Titus 3:8, 14 the RSV translates the word "to apply themselves." It is possible that Paul uses the word here to denote officials; it is also possible that he uses it to denote certain influential teachers among the Thessalonians. In view of verse 20, there is a strong likelihood that the men were prophets. Paul urged the Corinthians "to be subject to such men" as Stephanas "and to every fellow worker and laborer." He also urged them to "give recognition" to such men as Stephanas, Fortunatus, and Achaicus (1 Cor. 16:15ff.). At any rate, what these leaders were doing was by way of helping the church; they were providing leadership by their teaching and service; they were leading by the authority of Christ, seeking to carry out his will, or, as Paul expresses it, they were serving **in the Lord.** Thirdly, these leaders are described as being **those who admonish you.** This further indicates that they are teachers and spiritual advisers. The Greek construction has one definite article with the three participles, indicating that reference is made, not to three separate groups of leaders, but rather to different functions of the same group. It seems likely that the first term, **labor,** is more of a general term while the two follow-

¹³ and to esteem them very highly in love because of their
work. Be at peace among yourselves. ¹⁴ And we exhort you,
brethren, admonish the idle, encourage the fainthearted,
help the weak, be patient with them all.

---

ing terms more specifically define what the labor is. Leading and admonishing are thus seen as a part of the labor of
these men.

[13] Paul continues by beseeching the Thessalonians:
esteem them very highly in love. They are to hold in high
regard these men whose work Paul has just described in the
preceding verse. Moreover, they are not to look upon these
men as a group aloof from them whose leadership they
must follow because of the stern demands of authority;
rather, they are to regard them **highly in love.** This esteem
of members for their leaders does not arise out of deference
to personalities; it is **because of their work.** They render a
Christian service that is worthy of respect (cf. 1 Cor.
16:15ff.; Heb. 13:7). When leaders lead with the recognition that they are serving **in the Lord** and when members
hold such men in high **esteem in love,** a harmonious and
victorious church will be the result.

In addition to maintaining a right attitude toward their
leaders and thus promoting peace within the church, the
Thessalonians are urged: **be at peace among yourselves.**
Jesus had given a similar admonition to his disciples (Mark
9:50; cf. Matt. 5:9). Paul admonished other Christians in a
similar way (2 Cor. 13:11; Rom. 12:18). It is the obligation
of every Christian to seek peaceful relations with all other
Christians.

[14] Paul begins a new phase of his exhortations. Some
think that in verse 14 he turns from addressing the entire
group to address the leaders, but this does not seem likely.
It rather seems that he continues to speak to the entire
group of brethren that he has been addressing in the previous verses. Of course, the leaders would be expected to do
what Paul here enjoins, but it does not seem that he desires

that the activity be confined to them. The first admonition is: **admonish the idle.** The word translated **idle** was originally a military term and referred to a soldier's being out of step. Milligan discusses at length the use of the word in Hellenistic Greek to refer to idleness. There were idlers and loafers among the Thessalonians (cf. 2 Thess. 3:6ff.). Some think that Paul has in mind those who had lapsed into a state of idleness due to mistaken notions about the Lord's coming but there is no necessity for assuming this. The problem had evidently existed all along. Even while Paul was in Thessalonica he had given some rather strong teaching regarding work (2 Thess. 3:10). He desires that the members of the church show concern for these negligent members and that all have a part in the admonition.

Paul admonishes the Thessalonians regarding their treatment of various other groups within the church. **Encourage the fainthearted** is his next plea. There is the suggestion here that some were discouraged. Some were anxious and despondent. It may be that they were burdened by the death of friends or relatives or that they were fearful of persecution. Any number of causes could have produced such despondency, especially in the hearts of those who were not so bold and strong as others. The word **encourage** shows that Paul intends for gentleness and tenderness to be shown toward these. They need to know that others care and that others desire to help them bear their burdens. Christians must have sympathy for the **fainthearted.** Sympathy is also called for in the next exhortation: **help the weak.** The word from which **help** is translated literally means to "hold on to" or to "cling to." The **weak** are placed in a separate category from the **idle** and the **fainthearted,** and likely the spiritually weak are indicated—those who are more easily tempted to lapse into impurity. These are not to be surrendered to the evil forces; they are to be held up and strengthened. They are to have tender sympathy shown for them. They are to know that others are with them in the battle. In the next admonition

¹⁵ See that none of you repays evil for evil, but always seek to do good to one another and to all. ¹⁶ Rejoice always,

---

Paul turns from the specific needs of particular classes and points out a need of the entire church: **be patient with them all.** Every Christian is to manifest a gentle spirit and exercise forbearing patience toward all others. He must deny self and consider the good of others above his own personal desires.

[15] Paul continues his admonitions. He urges: **See that none of you repays evil for evil.** Here is a warning against revenge, against retaliation. The Christian is not to seek to "get even" with those who mistreat him. Instead, as the antithesis shows, he is to **seek to do good.** As the context shows, the good is that which is beneficial to the recipient. The Christian is to be habitually seeking for the good of others as is emphasized by the adverb **always.** And this habitual seeking for the good of others is not to be restricted **to one another** but is to reach out **to all.** Great concern is shown throughout the epistle for those outside the church (cf. 3:12; 4:12). This matter of forgiving others and of returning good for evil receives much emphasis in the New Testament. In a familiar passage in Romans (12:17) Paul insists upon the same high standard; the apostle Peter echoes the same plea (1 Peter 3:9). In the Sermon on the Mount Jesus himself had insisted that this attitude and conduct are to be characteristic of his disciples (Matt. 5:38ff.). Jesus not only taught the idea of repaying evil with good; he lived it out in his own life. His attitude during the mock trials through which he was hurried and his prayer on the cross for those who had crucified him were supreme demonstrations of the attitude he sought to instil in his disciples. Paul pleads for the Thessalonians to follow in the footsteps of their Lord.

[16] Having exhorted the Thessalonian Christians concerning their conduct toward others, Paul now turns to another area of the Christian life. **Rejoice always** he urges.

¹⁷ pray constantly,

Again, he uses the present imperative which means "keep on rejoicing." Paul has already referred to the joy of the Thessalonians in the midst of persecutions (1:6); he appealed to this as one proof of their having been chosen of God. He makes a similar appeal to the church at Philippi, another Macedonian church (Phil. 4:4). He claims rejoicing as a part of his own experience (2 Cor. 6:10). The true Christian can always find reason for rejoicing. He rejoices in the newness of life he has found in Christ and in the hope which he shares with other Christians. Even though he is experiencing sorrows and tears and is burdened with life's cares, he can rejoice beneath all these weights. His joy is not that which is born of outward conditions and circumstances. It is a joy existing in the depth of his heart because of his spiritual riches. He is in possession of treasures over which he can rejoice even in the midst of suffering. He can smile through his tears. He knows that because he is a Christian he is in possession of that which no one, not even death itself, can take from him (cf. Phil. 3:1, 1 Peter 4:13; Col. 1:24).

[17] Christian joy often finds expression in prayer and prayer is often the means by which obstacles are removed which stand in the way of joy. Especially in the midst of trials the heart feels the need of reaching outward for a closer fellowship with God. Paul admonishes: **pray constantly.** He does not mean for Christians to go about with the lips moving constantly and with words being incessantly uttered. He does mean for their souls to be constantly elevated to God and he means for prayer to be constant in the life of the Christian (cf. Rom. 12:12; Col. 4:2). Jesus taught the same thing when he urged his disciples "always to pray" (Luke 18:1). The Christian ever looks to God for guidance; he is ever conscious of his dependence on God. Though he does not constantly utter prayers, he is never to leave off praying.

¹⁸ give thanks in all circumstances; for this is the will of God in Christ Jesus for you. ¹⁹ Do not quench the Spirit,

---

[18] Paul next gives an admonition concerning thanksgiving: **give thanks in all circumstances.** Constant joy and constant prayer should lead to constant giving of thanks to God (cf. Eph. 5:20; Phil. 4:6; Col. 4:2f.). Paul is not saying that Christians are to give thanks for every event and circumstance in the world. He is saying that they should give thanks regardless of the **circumstances** in which they find themselves.

The Christian can always find something for which he can thank God. It is not enough that he feel thankful; he is to express his gratitude and heartfelt thanks. Paul's words, **for this is the will of God,** may refer only to the last of the admonitions, that concerning thanksgiving. However, it seems preferable to refer the words to the three admonitions of verses 16-18. It is God's will that Christians always rejoice, that they pray constantly, and that they give thanks to God in all of life's circumstances. It is **in Christ** that such is possible.

[19] In Paul's admonition, **Do not quench the Spirit,** he again makes use of the present imperative which means, "Do not continue to quench the Spirit." This indicates that some in the church at Thessalonica were doing what Paul here prohibits. The word **quench** is ordinarily used in the sense of extinguishing a fire (cf. Matt. 25:8; Mark 9:48). Evidently Paul is representing the Holy Spirit as a fire which can be extinguished. In several passages there is a close association of the Holy Spirit with fire (Acts 2:3; Rom. 12:11; 2 Tim. 1:6). Some (e.g., Lightfoot, Morris, Lenski) feel that the prohibition has somewhat of a wide application—that Paul is prohibiting the quenching of the Spirit by immorality, or hardness of heart, or carelessness, or by any course of life that is contrary to the will of God. It is true that the Holy Spirit in the heart can be quenched in these various ways. However, the present passage in its

[20] do not despise prophesying, [21] but test everything; hold fast what is good,

---

context seems to have a more limited application; it seems better to regard it (as do Ellicott, Robertson, Milligan, Frame) as prohibiting the repression and the disregard of the extraordinary operations (charismata) of the Holy Spirit (see 1 Cor. 12, 14 for the proper use of these spiritual gifts in edifying the church). Milligan suggests that perhaps some had a dread of overenthusiasm and were discouraging the use of the charismatic gifts.

[20] Frame's idea that from the prohibition against the repression of the use of the various spiritual gifts in verse 19, Paul now turns to discuss a particular spiritual gift, seems to be correct. Paul discusses the gift of prophecy, along with other spiritual gifts, in 1 Corinthians 14; he regards it as a most useful gift in the edification of the church. Prophets were men through whom God spoke and were next in importance to the apostles. "And his gifts were that some should be apostles, some prophets . . . (Eph. 4:11). Prophets played an important part in the delivering of God's will to man in the days of inspiration, the days of miraculous, spiritual, gifts. Evidently some among the Thessalonians had the tendency to underrate prophecy; they were not attaching the importance to the teachings of inspired prophets which those teachings deserved. The word translated **despise** means literally "to set at naught." Paul pleads with the Thessalonians not to set at naught these inspired messages. The fact that there were prophets in the church at Thessalonica makes it likely that the leaders previously mentioned were those of this class (see notes on vs. 12).

[21] In an adversative form Paul goes ahead to state the antithesis to the prohibition of verse 20. True prophecy is not to be despised; it is to be accepted and used. However, Paul urges the Thessalonians to **test everything**. He wants them to discriminate so as not to be misled by false

²² abstain from every form of evil.

---

prophets. One of the spiritual gifts was the ability to dis-
cern spirits (1 Cor. 12:10; cf. 14:29). Perhaps Paul is asking
that this gift be used. John issued a warning similar to
Paul's: "Beloved, do not believe every spirit, but test the
spirits to see whether they are of God; for many false
prophets have gone out into the world" (1 John 4:1). Paul
does not want the Thessalonians to accept everything
which claims to be prophetic without putting it to the
proper test.

But, with Paul, the testing is not all there is to it. He
presses upon his readers the fact that, after the testing, they
are to **hold fast what is good.** They are to hold to prophecy
that has been proved to be genuine. It is not enough to
decide what is of good quality. There must be an embrac-
ing of that which is good; there must be a tenacious hold-
ing fast to it. It is to be expected that, after the teaching has
been tested and has been proved to be good, those who see
that it is good will realize its true value and will cling to it
at all costs.

[22] In the final admonition of this section, Paul says:
abstain from every form of evil. The translation of the KJV,
"all appearance of evil," has caused some to misunderstand
what Paul is here saying. They have thought the prohibition to mean to abstain, not only from evil, but from anything which has the appearance of evil, that is, semblance
as opposed to reality. However, even with this rendering,
the word "appearance" does not have the idea of semblance
but rather that of outward or visible form. It is possible that
Paul is commanding abstinence from **evil** in whatever **form**
it appears; however, it seems more in keeping with the
context to consider the prohibition to refer to avoidance of
every **form** of false prophecy. Christians are exhorted to
hold to the good prophecy and to abstain from every **form**
of false or **evil** prophecy. Jesus warned against "false
prophets, who come to you in sheep's clothing, but in-

²³ May the God of peace himself sanctify you wholly; and
may your spirit and soul and body be kept sound and
blameless at the coming of our Lord Jesus Christ.

---

wardly are ravenous wolves" (Matt. 7:15; cf. 2 Cor. 11:13-
15).

Concluding Matters, 5:23–28

[23] In the benediction the writers give expression to a
prayer for the Thessalonians. It is not unusual to find
reference to the God of peace near the close of an epistle
(cf. Rom. 15:33; 16:20; 2 Cor. 13:11; Phil. 4:9; see also 2
Thess. 3:16). God is the source of true peace. The peace of
heart which Christians know has its origin in him. The
writers' prayer is that God may sanctify the Thessalonians
wholly. This is tantamount to praying that God will consecrate these Christians, set them apart for his service completely. It is a prayer that God will consecrate every part of
the entire being of every Christian. Sanctification may be
viewed as an act which took place at conversion. Hence
Paul could say to the Corinthians, "You were sanctified" (1
Cor. 6:11). He could describe these same people as "those
sanctified" (1 Cor. 1:2). But sanctification is not to be
considered as complete at this point. It is a process as may
be seen from Paul's prayer for the Thessalonian Christians.
As the Christian grows to higher levels of maturity, he
becomes more thoroughly consecrated or sanctified. The
goal of every Christian should be complete sanctification.
Sanctification involves the entirety of a person, not merely a
segment of him. In an earlier part of the epistle the writers
have told the Thessalonians that God's will for them is their
sanctification; moreover, they have gone into details as to
what is involved in living a life of sanctification (4:3ff.).

The writers continue their prayer for the Thessalonians.
They pray that the entire person—spirit, soul, and body—
will be kept sound or complete in all its parts; they pray
that the entire person—spirit, soul, and body—will be kept

²⁴ **He who calls you is faithful, and he will do it.**

---

blameless, that is, that it will be kept so that nothing blameworthy will be attached to it. The prayer, therefore, is for the sanctification and the preservation of these Christians. **At the coming of our Lord Jesus Christ** indicates that Paul and his helpers are praying that the Thessalonians will be found in this sanctified and kept condition at the time of the Lord's coming. To find **soul** and **spirit** mentioned in the same passage is not usual. Paul likely is not attempting to make a great distinction; he is intending to describe in graphic terms the entire man. If there is a distinction to be made, it may be that he intends by **spirit** to designate the nature which is akin to God; and that by **soul** he intends to designate the life which animates the body and which man shares in common with the animal creation. This section of the epistle ends with a prayer as did the first (3:11-13).

[24] The writers declare that God is the basis of their confidence. They describe him as **he who calls you**. The time when one heard the gospel and responded to it may be viewed as a time when God called him (2 Thess. 2:14). But the call of God continues to come to men through his word; hence he may appropriately be described as presently calling Christians. He calls them to a life of complete sanctification as the writers declare in the preceding verse. They affirm that the God **who calls is faithful**. Attention is here called to a characteristic of God which is emphasized throughout the Bible (cf. 1 Cor. 1:9; 2 Thess. 3:3; 1 Cor. 10:13; Heb. 10:23). He is not fickle nor whimsical. Upon him man can depend; he will fulfill his promises. **He will do it** the writers assure the Thessalonians. This is an assurance that God will do all that is contained in the substance of the prayer of verse 23—he will sanctify and he will keep. He not only calls; he will do all he possibly can do to bring that call to its completion. However, man must cooperate with God in the process of sanctification as can be seen from the instructions of 4:3ff. Furthermore, God's keeping a

123

²⁵ **Brethren, pray for us.** ²⁶ **Greet all the brethren with a holy kiss.**

Christian depends upon man's willingness to be kept and upon his keeping himself. "Keep yourselves in the love of God" (Jude 21). This admonition was given by one who affirmed that God "is able to keep you from falling" (Jude 24). The apostle Peter reminded Christians that they "by God's power are guarded through faith for a salvation ready to be revealed in the last time" (1 Peter 1:5). God's power will not keep a Christian who will not keep himself. Since Christians are kept "by faith," then the power of God will not keep those whose faith has been upset or overthrown (2 Tim. 2:18) nor those who have had shipwreck made of their faith (1 Tim. 1:19). God's keeping a Christian, then, is contingent upon that Christian's keeping of faith. If there is any failure, it will not be on God's part for **he is faithful;** it will be failure on the part of man.

[25] Paul, having expressed a prayer for the Thessalonians, asks them to remember him and his fellow workers in their prayers. It is not at all unusual for Paul to request the prayers of other Christians; this he does often (e.g., Rom. 15:30; Col. 4:3, 4; 2 Thess. 3:1, 2). In this request, Paul makes use of the present imperative emphasizing that he wants them to continue in such prayers.

[26] The writers urge, in verse 26: **Greet all the brethren with a holy kiss.** The kiss was a customary method of greeting. That it should be a genuine expression of Christian love is emphasized by the adjective **holy.** Paul makes reference to the **holy kiss** as a token of greeting in other passages (Rom. 16:16; 1 Cor. 16:20; 2 Cor. 13:12). Peter admonishes Christians to "Greet one another with a kiss of love" (1 Peter 5:14). The kiss as a token of greeting was used before Christianity came into being; Christians continued with the custom. It is clear, in such passages as Romans 16:16 and 1 Corinthians 16:20, that Paul is urging that the kiss be holy in reciprocal greetings among Chris-

²⁷ I adjure you by the Lord that this letter be read to all the brethren. ²⁸ The grace of our Lord Jesus Christ be with you.

---

tians. However, the construction of the present passage is different, and it seems preferable to take it to mean that the writers are asking the readers to greet one another for them. They include **all the brethren.** They do not want any individual to feel that he has been omitted from the greeting. They want even those whom they have felt compelled to rebuke to feel that they are included in this genuine expression of Christian greeting.

[27] Using the first person singular, Paul gives a rather strong injunction: **I adjure you by the Lord. Adjure** means "to cause to swear by." Paul is in substance saying that he is putting the Thessalonian brethren under oath. His deep sense of the importance of what he is asking them to do causes him to use this solemn adjuration. He urges the church, as a group, to see to it that all the brethren hear the reading of the epistle (cf. Col. 4:16). He would surely want those who were grieving about departed loved ones to hear the assurance of 4:13-18; he would surely want his expressions of concern and love to be heard by each and every member; in brief, he wants **all the brethren** to hear every word he has written.

[28] As his custom is, Paul closes the epistle with a prayer that **the grace of** the Lord may be with his readers. He had begun the epistle by expressing his desire for the grace of God to be with the Thessalonians (1:1). It is thus appropriate that, in the benediction of this epistle, he should again express his desire for the grace of God to be with his readers—that unmerited grace of God which is revealed and bestowed through **our Lord Jesus Christ.**

III

Introduction to 2 Thessalonians

On the city of Thessalonica and the establishment of the church there, see Introduction to 1 Thessalonians.

OCCASION OF 2 THESSALONIANS

THERE IS NO WAY of knowing all the events that intervened between the writing of 1 and 2 Thessalonians. But in some manner news reached Paul regarding conditions in Thessalonica after the writing of the first epistle. Some aspects of these conditions demanded immediate attention; hence Paul wrote the second epistle.

The first epistle had not been in vain. In it the church was praised for its steadfastness in the midst of trials, and it was exhorted to continue in such steadfastness, even to grow and abound in faith. The second epistle reveals that this admonition had been heeded. Also, it is noticeable that the vein of defense is absent from the second, indicating that Paul feels it to be needed no longer. The fears which the living had regarding the dead saints were evidently allayed since that point does not recur.

Paul and his colleagues still thank God for the growing faith of the Thessalonians, a faith that continued to grow in the midst of continuing persecutions (1:3-5). The writers feel that encouragement is still needed; they provide additional details of the judgment day at which time God's people will receive rest and their persecutors will receive vengeance (1:5-12).

Paul also writes to prevent the Thessalonians from being deceived and shaken by teaching which alleges that the day of the Lord has already arrived. Evidently some false teachers among the Thessalonians were causing disturbance. It may be that they were misusing something Paul had taught while he was in Thessalonica or something he had taught in the first epistle regarding the suddenness of the coming of the Lord (1 Thess. 5:1ff.). Or it may be that a rumor was being circulated purporting to have come from Paul (2 Thess. 2:2). To what extent the teaching was being received is not stated. But Paul has learned of the disturbance and he writes to correct the mistaken idea, reminding the Thessalonians of certain facts he had taught when in their midst. He knows that if they will recall certain things which he had taught must transpire they will know that the day of the Lord cannot yet have arrived. He refers to the "rebellion" and to the "man of lawlessness" as events to transpire before the arrival of the day of the Lord. Practically all of chapter 2 is devoted to this problem.

Paul has also heard that the idlers are giving trouble. It may be that speculations regarding the second coming had caused the problem to be intensified. Paul feels that the time has come for these offenders to be disciplined and the greater part of chapter 3 is devoted to this problem.

The purpose of 2 Thessalonians may be said to be fourfold: (1) to express gratitude for the steadfastness of the Thessalonians in the midst of trials; (2) to encourage the church to continue in steadfastness and in its fidelity to the teachings they had received; (3) to correct certain false ideas regarding the arrival of the day of the Lord; (4) to

127

admonish the disorderly within the church and to admonish the church as to its duties toward the disorderly ones.

AUTHORSHIP

The author claims to be Paul and there is no serious reason for questioning this (1:1; 3:17). He associates the names of Silvanus and Timothy with him in the greeting as he does in the first epistle, and the plural "we" is found as in the first. Silvanus and Timothy had had intimate association with the Thessalonians and this is probably the reason they are included with Paul in the greeting and why the letter is written in such a way as to show that they concur with Paul in what is said.

External evidence is stronger than for the first epistle. Second Thessalonians is included in the Muratorian Canon, the Old Syriac, the Old Latin, and in the Canon of Marcion. Polycarp quotes from 2 Thessalonians in a context in which he mentions Paul (c. A.D. 135; see Polycarp's *Epistle to the Philippians* XI, 3, 4; cf. III, 2). Justin Martyr evidently makes reference to 2 Thessalonians 2:3 in his *Dialogue with Trypho* CX. Irenaeus is the first of the patristic writers to mention the epistle by name and to ascribe it to Paul (*Against Heresies* III, 6, 5; 7, 2; IV, 27, 4; 29, 1; 33, 11). A contemporary of Irenaeus, Clement of Alexandria, who flourished A.D. 190-200, quotes 2 Thessalonians 3:1, 2 (*Stromata* V, 3).

As to internal evidence, the style and the vocabulary are genuinely Pauline. Some have felt that the similarities of 1 and 2 Thessalonians indicate the work of a forger who was attempting to make the second epistle seem genuinely Pauline. However, the similarities are accounted for by the fact that the writer is dealing with matters pertaining to the same general areas in both epistles. Moreover, the similarities have been exaggerated. Parallelism between the two cannot be seen in more than one-third of the entire contents and these often occur in greatly different connections. A close examination of the two epistles reveals that they are considerably different in content. The similarities suggest more the free handling of words and phrases by the same writer than the slavish copying of a forger.

Differences between 1 and 2 Thessalonians have been pointed out. Attention has been called by some to the fact that the first epistle, being clearly addressed to converts from paganism, has almost no allusions to the Old Testament, while the second, especially in its apocalyptic portion, alludes often to the Old Testament. Some have objected to Pauline authorship on the basis of differences in tone and vocabulary. Whatever differences in tone that are found in the epistle may be accounted for by the nature of the subject matter and by the fact that persistence of certain irregularities calls for regulations more stern and language more insistent. It is true that there are some words found only in 2 Thessalonians but only ten as compared with seventeen in the first epistle. The use of such words is easily accounted for by the treatment of such unique matters as are dealt with in the epistle.

Doctrinal differences between the two epistles with reference to the second coming of Christ have been alleged. It is said that in the first epistle that event is said to be near and there is no mention of precursory signs, while in the second epistle it is definitely affirmed that the coming of Christ will not occur until after certain events have transpired. It has been argued that these two ideas are mutually exclusive and that since Paul would not have changed his mind within so short a period of time the conclusion should be reached that the reference to precursory signs in the second epistle indicates a later writer. However, the apparent difference is due to a difference of emphasis. In apocalyptic passages signs and suddenness are not considered as contradictory. And the first epistle does not teach the imminency of the return of Christ—only the suddenness of the event. Moreover, it does not preclude the appearance of the "apostasy" and the "man of lawlessness" before the second coming of Christ.

Paul indicates in the second epistle that he had, while in Thessalonica, acquainted the Thessalonians with the precursory signs. When he wrote, in the first epistle, about the suddenness of the coming of Christ he knew they were already acquainted with the precursory signs. However, the second epistle does not teach a long delay before the revealing of the man of lawlessness. There is nothing in either epistle to preclude the possibility of the coming of Christ in that generation.

Difficulties connected with the alleged differences between 1 and 2 Thessalonians have been solved by some who have proposed that 2 Thessalonians was written first. Some of these have proposed that 2 Thessalonians was written first and sent to Jewish Christians in Thessalonica and that 2 Thessalonians 3:17 shows it to be the first letter of Paul to the Thessalonians. It has been suggested that matters pertaining to the idlers in the second epistle (3:6ff.) give a clearer insight into the meaning of passages pertaining to idlers in the first epistle (4:11, 12; 5:14). It is also suggested that perhaps the more severe discipline of the second epistle may have been followed by the less severe of the first.

Neither the theory of two different groups in Thessalonica as recipients of the two epistles nor that of the inverted order of the two epistles will bear up under investigation. Both epistles are addressed to the same group designated as "the church of the Thessalonians," and the writers deal with this same group throughout the epistles. Allusions to the Old Testament in the second epistle can be accounted for on the basis that there were some Jews in the Thessalonian church and that these allusions are part of the apocalyptic which Paul evidently had explained while he was in Thessalonica (2 Thess. 2:5). Also, in the second epistle, the writers make reference to what they had previously written (2:15); it is more likely that they refer to 1 Thessalonians than to a letter which has been lost. The passage in the second epistle, "Now concerning the coming of our Lord Jesus and our assembling to meet him" (2:1), seems clearly to be a reference to what had previously been written in the first epistle (4:13-18). Reference in the second letter to the growth of faith and love (1:3) advances beyond reference to the same subject in the first epistle (1:2, 3), and indicates answer to the prayer of the first epistle (3:12). Moreover, the insistence upon more severe discipline toward the offenders is just what would be expected in a later letter since the less severe treatment called for in the first letter had not achieved the desired results (cf. 1 Thess. 5:14 with 2 Thess. 3:6ff.). For additional notes on this section, see pp. 115f.

External evidence in favor of the genuineness of 2 Thessalonians is so strong and the style is so thoroughly Pauline, that the objections which have been raised are not strong enough to cast doubt on the Pauline authorship of the epistle.

PLACE AND DATE OF WRITING

Paul, Silvanus, and Timothy are still together at the time of the writing of 2 Thessalonians (1:1). After the ministry in Corinth (Acts 18), Timothy is known to have been with Paul again in Ephesus (Acts 19:22), but there is no evidence that the three were ever together again after the stay in Corinth. Silvanus disappears from the narrative in Acts between the ministry in Corinth and that in Ephesus. The same general conditions in the Thessalonian church reflected in the first epistle are reflected in the second. The place of writing, therefore, was Corinth, the city from which the first epistle had been written. It is not possible that a long period of time could have elapsed between the writing of the two epistles. The interval could have been only a few months at the longest. The date assigned for the first epistle, A.D. 51-52, cannot be far from wrong for the second.

VALUE OF 2 THESSALONIANS

The doctrines found in the first epistle are likewise found in the second though nothing new is added to some of them.

There is the same emphasis on God as Father (1:2; 2:16). He is viewed as the source of grace, peace, and love (1:2, 12; 3:5). The writers direct attention to God as the one to whom they feel they must give thanks (1:3; 2:13); they look to him as the author of comfort and hope (2:16); they regard him as the one who comforts and establishes his people (2:17). He is the true God who is not known by some (1:8); he it is who has chosen the Thessalonians for salvation (2:13); he can make them worthy of his call (1:11); he is the one whose judgment is righteous (1:5).

Second Thessalonians presents a high view of Christ. His name is united with that of the Father in such way as to give emphasis to his deity (1:1, 2, 12). The writers include Christ along with the Father in their prayer for comfort and confirmation of the Thessalonians (2:16, 17). He will be revealed in glory at his second coming and will take vengeance upon those who do not obey him (1:8). He will destroy the man of lawlessness at his coming (2:8). He is described as Lord (e.g., 1:1, 2, 7, 8, 9, 12, ; 2:1, 8, 14, 16; 3:6, 12), the common term for God among the Jews of that day. The writers enforce their charges through Christ (3:6, 12).

It was pointed out in the Introduction to the first epistle that there is no elaborate view of the Holy Spirit in the Thessalonian letters. The second epistle adds the item that sanctification is accomplished by the Spirit (2:13).

Regarding salvation, the believer is said to exist in the realm of God and of Christ (1:1). Salvation was in God's purpose from the beginning; he purposed to save "through

132

sanctification of the Spirit and belief in the truth" (2:13). God calls to this salvation through the gospel (2:14). The Lord who saved will continue to strengthen and guard (3:3).

The second epistle, as the first, gives emphasis to the second coming and related events. Jesus will return from heaven to grant rest to his people and to take vengeance on others (1:5-10). The day of the Lord has not already come and the Thessalonians are not to be disturbed by any reports to that effect. There are certain events which must transpire before that day: the rebellion and the revelation of the man of lawlessness. When Jesus comes he will defeat this great enemy (2:1-12).

Emphasis on Christian virtues and on moral and ethical conduct continues in the second epistle. Brotherly love is encouraged (1:3); increasing faith is commended (1:3); obedience to the commandments is enjoined (2:15; 3:4). Faithful endurance in suffering afflictions and persecutions is for the purpose of making Christians worthy of the eternal kingdom (1:5). Christians are to live in calmness as opposed to excitement and anxiety and are to be on guard against deception of any sort (2:2, 3). Good words and good works are to be characteristic of the Christian (2:17). Honest toil is emphasized; living at the expense of others is condemned (3:7-11). Faithful Christians are to take note of the idlers and the busybodies and are to exercise corrective discipline (3:6, 14, 15). Admonitions in a spirit of brotherly love are to be continued toward these offenders (3:15).

Another value of 2 Thessalonians is the insight it gives as to Paul's oral teaching in Thessalonica. Chief in this respect is the information given in chapter 2 concerning the details Paul had given regarding the events to transpire before the arrival of the day of the Lord.

Furthermore, the second epistle, as the first, reveals the attitude and feeling of Paul toward his converts. They are still a source of joy to him. His life is bound up with theirs. His peace of mind is contingent upon their behavior. He does not despair of saving the church from its difficulties and problems even after repeated warnings and admonitions relative to the same problem. The Thessalonian Christians are his beloved brothers for whom he continually prays and whose prayers he desires on his own behalf.

OUTLINE

I. ENCOURAGEMENT, CHAPTER 1
   A. Salutation, 1:1, 2
   B. Thanksgiving, 1:3, 4
   C. The Righteous Judgment of God, 1:5-10
   D. Prayer, 1:11, 12

II. INSTRUCTION, CHAPTER 2
   A. Day of the Lord not already present, 2:1, 2
   B. Events to precede the day of the Lord: the rebellion and the revelation of the man of lawlessness, 2:3-12
   C. Thanksgiving and admonition, 2:13-15
   D. Prayer for the Thessalonians, 2:16, 17

III. EXHORTATION, CHAPTER 3
   A. Exhortation to pray for the writers, 3:1, 2
   B. Expression of confidence in the Lord and in the Thessalonians, 3:3-5
   C. Exhortation concerning treatment of disorderly members, 3:6-15
   D. Conclusion, 3:16-18

COMPARISON OF THE STRUCTURE OF 1 AND 2 THESSALONIANS

A comparison of the two epistles, 1 and 2 Thessalonians, reveals a remarkable similarity in structural pattern. It is a similarity which might be expected in two letters coming from the same writer and addressed to the same church over a short period of time. Yet there are also differences between the two. However, these differences are due to the special concerns of the two letters. The following table indicates the similarities and also places where the structural pattern is different.

Comparison

1 THESSALONIANS		2 THESSALONIANS
1:1	Salutation	1:1, 2
1:2, 3	Thanksgiving	1:3
1:4-8	Congratulations	1:4

At this point a break in the pattern can be seen, but that which breaks the pattern is indicative of the special concern in each epistle. In the first epistle the missionaries discuss their conduct and reception in Thessalonica and other personal matters which appear to be for the purpose of some type of defense (1:9-3:10). In the second epistle the missionaries discuss the righteous judgment of God (1:5-10) and events which will precede the coming of Christ (2:1-15). The parallels are later resumed.

3:11-13	Petitions regarding special needs of readers	1:11f.; 2:16f.
4:1-5:11	Practical instructions, with each section introduced by "finally"	3:1ff.
5:23	Benediction	3:16
5:26	Greeting	3:17
5:28	Benediction	3:18

IV

The Second Letter of Paul to the Thessalonians

ENCOURAGEMENT, CHAPTER 1

SECOND THESSALONIANS may be considered as having three divisions, each chapter a division. Chapter 1 is devoted largely to matters of an encouraging nature.

The writers greet the readers and express their gratitude for the spiritual state of the Thessalonian church. They are thankful for the growing faith and the abounding love; they can therefore boast among other churches of the steadfastness of the Thessalonians (1:1-4).

Paul and his helpers assure the Thessalonians that their conduct is evidence of God's righteous judgment and that by endurance they may be made worthy of God's kingdom. God will recompense with affliction those who are persecuting the Thessalonians, and he will grant rest to those being afflicted. This will be at the time the Lord returns. Paul next elaborates upon the punishment of the unrighteous and the glory awaiting the saints at the time of the Lord's coming (1:5-10).

¹ Paul, Silvanus, and Timothy, To the church of the Thessalonians in God our Father and the Lord Jesus Christ: ² Grace to you and peace from God the Father and the Lord Jesus Christ.

The writers assure the Thessalonians of their constant prayers in their behalf; they pray that God will make them worthy of his call and that he will enable them to complete their resolutions and their works of faith. They pray for this so that the name of Christ may be glorified in the Thessalonians and that the Thessalonians may be glorified in Christ (1:11, 12).

Everything in chapter 1, from the warm greeting to the prayer, is of a nature as to be encouraging to a troubled church.

Salutation, 1:1, 2

[1] The names of the same three are united and the church is described in much the same way as in the first epistle (see notes on 1 Thess. 1:1). The one difference is that **God** is here designated **our Father** rather than "the Father." God is at times called "Father" in relation to Jesus (e.g., Rom. 15:6; 2 Cor. 1:3; 11:31); at times he is designated "Father" in relation to his people (e.g., Rom. 1:7; 1 Cor. 1:3; 2 Cor. 1:2). It is in the latter sense that the term is here used; the use of **our** emphasizes the fact that the writers and the readers have a common **Father** and are united in a common family.

[2] The greeting is longer than the greeting in the first letter (see notes on 1 Thess. 1:1). **From God the Father and the Lord Jesus Christ** is added (cf. Rom. 1:7; 1 Cor. 1:3; 2 Cor. 1:2). This specifies both Father and Son as the source of **grace** and **peace,** the common source. The names of the two are associated in the closest possible fashion (see notes on 1 Thess. 1:1).

³ **We are bound to give thanks to God always for you, brethren, as is fitting, because your faith is growing abundantly, and the love of every one of you for one another is increasing.**

Thanksgiving, 1:3, 4

[3] The only two instances in which Paul uses the expression, **we are bound,** in thanksgiving are here and 2:13. He feels a sense of obligation to God, an impelling urgency **to give** thanks for the spiritual progress of the Thessalonians. **We are bound** expresses personal obligation (cf. Rom. 13:8 where the same word is translated "owe"). On the expression, **thanks to God always,** see p. 26.

Thanksgiving is not only an expression which the writers feel they owe to God; they assure the readers that they deserve the commendation implied by such thanksgiving. **As is fitting** indicates the appropriateness of the thanksgiving. The writers, by such thanksgiving, acknowledge the true state of the Thessalonians. They acknowledge that the progress of the Thessalonians in the face of persecution causes such thanksgiving to be in order.

With **because** the writers proceed to explain why they feel compelled to thank God and why such thanksgiving is in order: first, **because your faith is growing abundantly.** Paul had before spoken of something "lacking in your faith" (1 Thess. 3:10). He has since learned that their faith **is growing;** the word **abundantly** indicates that it was growing immeasurably. Next, the thanksgiving is because **the love of every one of you for one another is increasing.** The writers had previously prayed that the love of these Christians would abound (1 Thess. 3:12). Now they express gratitude that God has answered the prayer. The phrase, **every one of you for one another,** indicates that the love was not merely general but was individually manifested. This passage reveals an exuberance of joy and gratitude on the part of the writers.

The triad of 1 Thessalonians 1:3 is not repeated here—hope is not specified. Some commentators (e.g., Bailey) make no mention of the fact that hope is here omitted. Frame mentions the difference between the two epistles at this point; however, he sees significance in the fact that Paul wishes to call special attention to their love for each other since he had given such special emphasis to such love in the first epistle (cf. 4:9, 10; 3:12). Commenting on verse 4, Lightfoot says that *hupomonē* (steadfastness, RSV) is usually found in conjunction with hope (as 1 Thess. 1:3) but that it is here connected with faith, and that a sharp line of distinction between the two is not easily drawn. Lenski says the omission of hope from the passage is due to the fact that some in Thessalonica had misconstrued the true doctrine of hope and had also changed their way of living. Hendriksen disagrees with this position, maintaining that it is an error to infer from the omission of hope that Paul felt that the Thessalonians had lost hope. Morris says the omission is probably not significant since Paul does not indicate that the Thessalonians are deficient in hope.

It seems best to conclude, with Morris and Hendriksen, and evidently with those that make no mention of the omission of hope from verse 3 or mention it only for comparative purposes, that the omission is not necessarily significant. It is doubtless true that the hope of some of the Thessalonians was deficient. But there were some deficiencies in the hope of some of them when Paul wrote the first epistle wherein he expressed gratitude for their "steadfastness of hope" (1:3). If some had become convinced that the day of the Lord had come by the time Paul wrote the second letter, it is not made clear just what they thought had already occurred nor what they thought was yet to occur. Had they given up hope for the resurrection of friends and relatives? Nothing is said to that effect. Whatever deficiency existed regarding the arrival of the day of the Lord, it does not seem likely that it existed among the greater part of the church.

⁴ Therefore we ourselves boast of you in the churches of
God for your steadfastness and faith in all your persecutions and in the afflictions which you are enduring.

---

[4] With **therefore** the writers proceed to state the result of the increasing love and faith of the Thessalonians. In
consequence of such love and faith Paul boasts of them
among other churches (cf. 1 Thess. 1:8; 2:19). Reference is
likely made to the church in Corinth, where the writers
were at the time of writing, and also to other churches of
the area (cf. 2 Cor. 8:1; 9:2). The two particular virtues
were **steadfastness and faith** (cf. 1 Thess. 1:3). **Steadfastness** indicates an active and heroic constancy. **Faith** points
to their trust in God and their reliance upon him. What was
especially remarkable about the **steadfastness** and the **faith**
of the Thessalonians was that they were manifested **in all
your persecutions and in the afflictions which you are enduring.** In the first epistle mention is made of their having
"received the word in much affliction" (1:6), and of their
suffering at the hands of their own countrymen (2:14). The
present tense, **you are enduring,** shows that their sufferings
are continuing right up to the time the letter is being
written. **Persecutions** is a term that is somewhat specific,
indicating sufferings from external sources brought on because of their faith. **Afflictions** is a more general term and
refers to difficult trials of various sorts (cf. 2 Cor. 8:2). It
likely includes the mental anguish which comes as a result
of persecutions and may continue after the persecutions
have ended. Other passages which mention both persecutions and afflictions or tribulations together are Matthew
13:21 and Mark 4:17. The endurance and the faith of the
Thessalonians had held up even in the midst of such adversities (cf. Rev. 1:9). Of this the writers can boast among
the churches; for this they can rejoice.

The significance of the emphatic, **we ourselves,** is not
clear. Frame supposes certain faint-hearted ones in Thessalonica had, in a letter, remonstrated by saying that they

⁵ **This is evidence of the righteous judgment of God, that you may be made worthy of the kingdom of God, for which you are suffering—**

---

were not worthy of the praise given in the first epistle. He thinks the emphatic expression, **we ourselves,** is in contrast with what Paul thought certain Thessalonians would have said or would have expected him to say. Morris thinks the emphatic expression is due to the fact that it was unusual for the founders of a church to boast of its accomplishments; yet the Thessalonian church was so outstanding for its steadfastness and faith that even the founders felt constrained to praise it in this manner. Lightfoot makes practically the same suggestion, adding that ordinarily the writers would be hesitant to such boasting lest it be thought that they were boasting of their own accomplishments. Lenski thinks the import to be that the writers themselves as well as others who know about the Thessalonian church boast of their spiritual qualities. Ellicott makes practically the same suggestion adding that the others might be among the Thessalonians or elsewhere. This latter seems to be the most likely significance; in the first epistle Paul had spoken of the far-reaching fame of the Thessalonian church (1:8, 9).

The Righteous Judgment of God, 1:5–10

[5] Verse 5 introduces the theme for the remainder of the chapter—the certainty of God's plan. Paul is seeking to give the Thessalonians a feeling of security by, in effect, elaborating upon the Christian's hope. To endure persecutions and afflictions in faith seems a hardship when viewed from a human standpoint; however, such endurance **is evidence of the righteous judgment of God.** The word **this** seems to be in apposition with the entire foregoing sentence, referring to the endurance of the Thessalonians— their patient endurance in adversity. The fact that they have been able thus to bear trials is proof that God is with

⁶ since indeed God deems it just to repay with affliction
those who afflict you,

---

them and is strengthening them; moreover, it is an indication that he will continue to see them through all other
adversities and will do all things in a way that is right. **The
righteous judgment of God** indicates the final day of judgment as the verses following clearly show. God's judgment
on that day will be a righteous judgment (cf. Rom. 2:5).
The faithful endurance of the Thessalonians in the midst of
adversities is regarded as evidence that God's judgment
will be righteous. Their ability to endure indicates the
presence of God; God's presence is assurance that he will
continue to be with them and will eventually adjust the
inequities of this life. The fact that God equips his people
to endure hardships indicates that he is righteous and will
manifest this righteousness in the end (cf. Matt. 5:10, 11).

The endurance and faith of the Thessalonians in the
midst of suffering is viewed as a part of God's providence in
working out his purpose: **that you may be made worthy of
the kingdom of God.** The New Testament teaches that
suffering does something for the people of God. "Suffering
produces endurance, and endurance produces character"
(Rom. 5:3, 4). There is thus a redemptive aspect to suffering. There is a refining process to be seen in the faithful
bearing of trials (1 Peter 1:6, 7; 4:12, 13). This does not
lend support to the idea of meritorious righteousness on the
part of man for it is God who, upon the basis of what Christ
has done, supplies grace for man's deficiencies and enables
him to endure sufferings (cf. 1 Thess. 2:12 and comments
there; Eph. 4:1; Phil. 1:27f.; Col. 1:9-12; Lk. 20:35). It is for
the sake of the **kingdom** that Christians suffer: **for which
you are suffering** (cf. Matt. 25:34; 2 Peter 1:11).

[6] The writers begin a discussion of the judgment of
those who persecute Christians. They point to the principle
of recompense; they affirm that retribution is inevitable.
Vengeance belongs to God and he will repay (see Rom.

⁷ and to grant rest with us to you who are afflicted, when
the Lord Jesus is revealed from heaven with his mighty
angels in flaming fire,

12:19 for the same word, "repay"). God's righteousness
demands that he condemn the sinner; his repaying with
affliction those who afflict his people is demanded by justice. The day of judgment will be a time when it will be
seen that God is righteous; his "righteous judgment will be
revealed" (Rom. 2:5).

[7] Continuing the thought of the righteous judgment
of God, the writers proceed to show that there is another
aspect to it: to grant rest. The word rest denotes freedom
from tensions; it is used in the New Testament only by Paul
and always in contrast with afflictions (cf. 2 Cor. 2:13; 7:5;
8:13). The New Testament teaches that "there remains a
sabbath rest for the people of God" (Heb. 4:9; cf. Rev.
14:13). Paul promises the afflicted Thessalonians that God
will grant rest to them; he says with us, including the
writers (see notes on 1 Thess. 4:17). Paul knew what it was
to be under tension; he had experienced such at Thessalonica and other places. The placing of the writers alongside
the readers in the experiencing of such afflictions and in the
sharing of rest shows the unity the writers felt with the
readers (cf. 1 Cor. 4:8; 2 Cor. 7:3; 1 Thess. 2:18-20). To
know that they are not alone in sufferings nor in anticipation of rest from afflictions will be of encouragement to the
Thessalonians. In the expression, to you who are afflicted, a
present participle is used showing that Paul knows that the
afflictions are in progress even as he writes.

The writers go ahead to explain just when the righteous
judgment of God will take place: when the Lord Jesus is
revealed from heaven. This refers to the second coming of
Christ, a subject mentioned in every chapter of 1 Thessalonians. However, the word *parousia* is not used here; the
word used is "revelation" (Greek, *apokalupsis*). It is a word
used often in eschatological contexts such as those which

⁸ inflicting vengeance upon those who do not know God
and upon those who do not obey the gospel of our Lord
Jesus.

---

speak of the revelation of the following: the glory of Christ
(1 Peter 4:13; 5:1); Christ himself (Luke 17:30; 1 Cor. 1:7;
1 Peter 1:7, 13); the righteous judgment of God (Rom. 2:5;
cf. 1 Cor. 3:13); the glory to be revealed to Christians
(Rom. 8:18f.; cf. Col. 3:4; 1 Peter 4:13); the appearance of
the lawless one and his subsequent defeat (2 Thess. 2:3, 6,
8). The word denotes a disclosing or a revealing. Though
the Lord is not now seen by his people, there will come a
time when he will be revealed visibly. He will be disclosed
to humanity. "And every eye shall see him" (Rev. 1:7).

Paul describes the revelation of Christ in three prepositional phrases. **From heaven** has reference to the place. In
the first epistle the Thessalonians are said to have turned to
God to serve him "and to wait for his Son from heaven"
(1:10). This has reference to the visible descent of Christ
(cf. Acts 1:11; 1 Thess. 4:16). The second phrase, **with his
mighty angels,** refers to the attendants of the Lord (see
notes on 1 Thess. 3:13; cf. Matt. 13:41, 42; 25:31). That
these are powerful, able to do the bidding of the Lord, is
indicated by **mighty.** Paul does not mention "the archangel's call" in the present connection (see notes on 1 Thess.
4:16). The third phrase, **in flaming fire,** points out another
accompaniment. The glory and the majesty of the coming
are thus emphasized (cf. Ex. 3:2; Acts 7:30; Isa. 66:15, 16; 2
Peter 3:10). The entire picture of the descending Lord is
tremendously mighty and majestic.

[8] The writers speak of the Lord's work of administer-
ing justice at the time he descends. The word **vengeance** is
from the same root as the word "righteous" (vs. 5) and the
word "just" (vs. 6). The idea is the administration of justice, not that of vindictive retaliation. The word from which
vengeance comes is translated "vindicate" (Luke 18:7) and
"punishment" (2 Cor. 7:11).

⁹ They shall suffer the punishment of eternal destruction and exclusion from the presence of the Lord and from the glory of his might,

---

It is possible that the expression, **those who do not know God,** refers to the pagan world (cf. Jer. 10:25; 1 Thess. 4:5). "They did not see fit to acknowledge God" (Rom. 1:28). Theirs was a wilful refusal to know God (Rom. 1:18-32; cf. Eph. 4:18, 19). It is possible that a second group is designated as **those who do not obey the gospel** (cf. 1 Peter 4:17). Some see in this a reference to the Jews. However, it is not certain that Paul had two distinct groups in mind. It may be that Paul is employing Hebrew parallelism. The passage could be translated: "those who do not know God, even upon those who do not obey the gospel." Jesus accused certain Jews of not knowing God (John 8:55) and Paul spoke of the Gentiles as being disobedient (Rom. 11:30). It is not a certainty, then, that Paul had two distinct groups in mind. Or, if he did, it is not certain that he referred, in the first, exclusively to Gentiles and, in the second, exclusively to Jews. Paul later spoke of "those who are to perish" as one group (2:10). The principal truth is not affected by the view one takes. The Lord will take **vengeance upon those who do not know God;** he will take vengeance **upon those** who do not accept the Lord in gospel obedience.

[9] The word **punishment** is another word from the same root as "righteous," "just," and "vengeance" of the preceding verses. It indicates the proceedings of justice and considers punishment from the viewpoint of the unbiased judge. **Punishment** is described as **destruction.** The idea of cessation of existence is not in the word. It is translated "ruin" in 1 Timothy 6:9 and is there used with another word (*apōleian*) which is translated "destruction." Paul also used the word in 1 Thessalonians 5:3. The words, **and exclusion** (RSV), are not in the Greek. However, the idea of exclusion is in the word **destruction** as can be seen from

¹⁰ **when he comes on that day to be glorified in his saints, and to be marveled at in all who have believed, because our testimony to you was believed.**

---

the fact that it is **from the presence of the Lord and from the glory of his might** (cf. Isa. 2:19; 59:17; 66:15f.). Exclusion from the Lord would be especially meaningful to Christians whose hope is to be with the Lord (cf. 1 Thess. 4:17 and notes; 2 Cor. 4:14; Col. 3:4). In the teaching of Jesus, separation was an aspect of punishment (Matt. 25:41).

Destruction will be **eternal** (*aiōnion*), a word which literally means "age-long." Duration of punishment will thus depend upon the length of the age and the New Testament indicates that it will be an age without end. Jesus used the word to refer to "eternal punishment" and "eternal life" (Matt. 25:46). Punishment of the wicked and life of the righteous will be of the same duration—forever. **Eternal destruction** is the very opposite of eternal life. To enjoy eternal life is to live forever in the presence of the Lord; to suffer eternal punishment involves being separated from the presence of the Lord (cf. Matt. 7:23). Further, it means separation **from the glory of his might** (cf. Isa. 2:10ff.). The mightiness of the Lord will be revealed to his people as they behold his glory. Those who are banished from his presence will be deprived of this blessed experience. Thus the "affliction" of verse 6 is vividly described.

[10] **When he comes on that day,** the day of the second coming, the *parousia,* specifies the time when the wicked will suffer the punishment of eternal destruction. The Greek has "whenever" with the aorist subjunctive, a construction indicating the certainty of the event and yet the uncertainty of the time of it. "That day" in the first epistle refers to the second coming of Christ (5:4).

After the expression, **when he comes,** there are two infinitives expressing purpose. First, Jesus will come **to be glorified in his saints** (cf. Col. 3:4). The glory of Christ will be seen reflected in his people—those who have been set

¹¹ To this end we always pray for you, that our God may make you worthy of his call, and may fulfil every good resolve and work of faith by his power,

---

apart by God for his service. They are an exhibition of his power and goodness; they demonstrate the power of the Lord in their lives; they, to a degree, manifest the characteristics of the Lord who transformed them. "Glory" is very important in Paul's writings. He speaks of the glory to be revealed to Christians (Rom. 8:18f.; Col. 3:4; cf. 1 Pet. 4:13). He writes of Christians sharing in the glory of Christ (Rom. 8:17; 1 Cor. 2:7; Phil. 3:21; Col. 1:27). Yet Paul does not think of glory entirely in terms of the coming of Christ; he thinks of Christians as already sharing the glory of the Lord and as growing in glory as they live in relationship with Christ (2 Cor. 3:15-18; 4:4-6). Second, Jesus will come **to be marveled at in all who have believed.** The word **saints** gives emphasis to the fact that these are sanctified ones, sanctification being the work of God; the designation, **all who have believed,** seems to give emphasis to the human activity involved in salvation (cf. 2:13f.). When believers see their Lord (see 1 John 3:2), they will be filled with wonder and awe. They will reflect his glory and will marvel at the glory which they see in him. This is in vivid contrast with the fate of unbelievers who will be excluded from the Lord's presence and glory (vs. 9).

Paul adds **because our testimony to you was believed.** This places the Thessalonians among those who will marvel at the Lord. Paul may intend this as a word of encouragement, especially for the "fainthearted" ones (1 Thess. 5:14). He is referring to the preaching which the Thessalonians had heard (see Acts 17:1-4; 1 Thess. 2:13).

Prayer, 1:11, 12

[11] Paul often turns from thanksgiving to petition (cf. 1 Thess. 3:11-13; Phil. 1:9-11; Col. 1:9-12). He encourages the Thessalonians by assuring them that he and his co-

¹² so that the name of our Lord Jesus may be glorified in you, and you in him, according to the grace of our God and the Lord Jesus Christ.

---

workers always pray for them. Specifically they pray that God may make them worthy of his call. On the expression "make worthy," see notes on verse 5 and on 1 Thessalonians 2:12. That for which they pray requires more than human strength; hence the prayer that God will help the Thessalonians to attain this high goal. Further, they pray that God may fulfil every good resolve and work of faith by his power. Every good resolve designates the resolutions or desires which spring from goodness. Goodness is one aspect of the fruit of the Spirit (Gal. 5:22). The Holy Spirit exerts an influence through the gospel which produces goodness in the believer's heart. This goodness causes the believer to have good resolutions. Paul prays that these resolutions may be completed, showing that he realizes man's need for divine help in the carrying out of good resolutions. Paul also prays that God may fulfil every work of faith. True faith produces works (see notes on 1 Thess. 1:3). This, too, is something man does. Yet he is motivated by God and God is seen as the source of faith. Man needs the help of God as he seeks to work his will. Paul is praying that God, by his power, will help the readers to complete every high resolve and every work of faith. At every turn Paul shows his realization of man's dependence upon God in bringing to completion his good resolutions and his works of faith.

[12] Paul states the purpose he has for praying the prayer of verse 11. First, it is so that the name of our Lord Jesus may be glorified in you, and you in him. Jesus, speaking to the Father said: "All mine are thine and thine are mine, and I am glorified in them" (John 17:10). In the same prayer he said: "The glory which thou hast given me I have given to them, that they may be one even as we are one" (vs. 22). When men accept Christ and live by his teachings, his name is glorified in them. The work of Jesus

in human hearts glorifies his name (cf. Gal. 1:24). A man's product which bears his name, if it is a good product, will bring honor to his name. Too, the man's name, if it is well known and honorable, brings honor to the product. Good students bring honor to the name of their teacher; in turn, the name of a great teacher brings honor to students. Paul feels that the relation of Christians to the Lord is such that, if they fulfil his desires for them, there will be a reciprocal sharing of glory. All of this is **according to the grace of God and the Lord,** or in accordance with that grace, for it is in divine grace that all such glorification finds its source. This reciprocal glorification occurs in this life wherever true Christians are found; it will find its complete fulfilment at the time of the Lord's coming (cf. notes on 1:10).

INSTRUCTION, CHAPTER 2

The writers state, in chapter 2, that they are writing about the coming of the Lord so that the Thessalonians will not be disturbed. They mention possible causes of disturbance such as a letter purporting to be from Paul wherein certain things were taught. The doctrine evidently being taught that was causing trouble was that the day of the Lord was already present (2:1, 2).

Paul warns the readers against being deceived; he assures them that the day of the Lord will not come until "the rebellion" takes place and "the man of lawlessness" is revealed—events about which he had told them when in their midst. He describes the blasphemous character of the man of lawlessness, but declares that he will not be revealed until that which restrains is out of the way. After he has been revealed, the Lord will come and bring him to utter defeat (2:3-12).

Paul and his helpers express thanks for the Thessalonian brethren—thanks that God has chosen them for salvation. It was for this that God had called them through the

¹ Now concerning the coming of our Lord Jesus Christ and our assembling to meet him, we beg you, brethren, ² not to be quickly shaken in mind or excited, either by spirit or by word, or by letter purporting to be from us, to the effect that the day of the Lord has come.

---

gospel. The writers admonish the readers to stand firm and to hold fast to what they had taught them (2:13-15).

In the closing verses of the chapter the writers express a prayer that Jesus and the Father may comfort and establish the Thessalonians (2:16, 17).

Day of the Lord not Already Present, 2:1, 2

[1] The writers had spoken in the first epistle of the coming of the Lord Jesus Christ and our assembling to meet him (4:13-18; 5:1-3). Events in Thessalonica since that epistle make further teaching necessary. It is possible that emphasis on the suddenness of the Lord's coming in the first epistle had been misinterpreted by some and they had become convinced of an imminent coming. It seems that some in Thessalonica were insisting that the day of the Lord was already present. To what extent the idea was being accepted in the church is not stated. Nor is it clear just what was believed by those who thought the day had already arrived. Certain details such as what they thought the day included (cf. 2 Tim. 2:18) and what they thought was yet to happen are not stated.

The writers use a strong word which has within it the idea of requesting or imploring. They beg the brethren in regard to the matter which they introduce.

[2] Paul is pleading for the Thessalonians not to lose their balance. To accept the teaching that the day of the Lord had already arrived would cause one to be shaken in mind and would leave him in an excited or agitated condition. The writers beg the Thessalonians to keep their heads in the midst of fanatical notions.

Paul discusses the possible means which could cause the

³ Let no one deceive you in any way; for that day will not
come, unless the rebellion comes first, and the man of
lawlessness * is revealed, the son of perdition,
* Other ancient authorities read *sin*

---

readers to be shaken in mind. **By spirit** refers to a communication through a prophet. Possibly Paul has in mind the
false prophets who pretend to speak by divine inspiration
(cf. 1 Thess. 5:19ff.; 1 John 4:1). **By word** refers to an oral
communication. **By letter** has reference to an epistle such as
Paul has previously written and is now writing. It is difficult to determine whether the expression, **purporting to be
from us,** goes only with **letter,** or with **word** and **letter,** or
with all three—**spirit, word,** and **letter.** Paul may refer to a
teacher who claimed divine revelation by the word **spirit**
and to sermons and lessons presented by **word.** Then, **purporting to be from us** qualifies **letter.** Perhaps some claimed
a letter from Paul. Or it is possible that Paul uses the
expression, **purporting to be from us,** meaning that the
Thessalonians are not to be shaken by reports of a revelation, or by rumors of oral teaching, or by claims of a letter
—as coming from him. Regardless of the view taken, the
resultant meaning is not affected. Paul begs the Thessalonians not to be shaken by such false ideas.

Events to Precede the Coming of the Lord, 2:3–12

[3] In verse 2, Paul mentioned possible ways by which
the Thessalonians might be deceived—spirit, word, or letter. He continues to plead: **Let no one deceive you in any
way.** The particular point about which he is pleading concerns the day of the Lord (see notes on 1 Thess. 5:2). He
does not want the Thessalonians to be deceived into thinking that it has already arrived.

The writers support their claim that the day has not
occurred by referring to events which must take place
before that time. They use apocalyptic imagery in their
descriptions, much of which is found in Jewish apocalyptic

⁴ who opposes and exalts himself against every so-called god or object of worship, so that he takes his seat in the temple of God, proclaiming himself to be God.

---

literature. On the nature of apocalyptic literature see the discussion at the end of this section.

The writers say **the rebellion** must come first, clearly implying that it has not yet come. The Greek word for rebellion, *apostasia,* indicates a defection from the faith which amounts to active opposition against it. The noun form is found only here and in Acts 21:21 where it refers to the forsaking of Moses by the Jews. The verb form denotes departure from the faith (1 Tim. 4:1) and a falling away from the true God (Heb. 3:12). In the Septuagint the noun form indicates "rebellion" (Josh. 22:22) and "the apostasy" which Antiochus Epiphanes was said to be enforcing (1 Macc. 2:15). In the present connection the writers seem to contemplate a falling away from God to the extent that open rebellion is the outcome. They do not indicate how widespread it will be, but they speak of it in such way, **the rebellion,** as to imply that they are writing about something of which they know the readers are aware.

Another event to precede the day of the Lord is the revealing of **the man of lawlessness.** The expression indicates that **the man** belongs to a lawless class or condition. The word for **revealed,** indicating an open manifestation, is used in 1:7 concerning the revelation of Jesus. **Son of perdition** is the exact term used by Jesus to describe Judas (John 17:12). **Son of** signifies belonging to or characterized by (see notes on 1 Thess. 5:3). It implies that he is destined for doom. As to the identity of the man of lawlessness, see special note at the end of this section.

[4] Two participial clauses connected with a single definite article continue the description of the man of lawlessness. He **opposes and exalts himself. . . .** The participles are present, indicating that his actions are not single acts but a continuing activity. He is an adversary, an active

⁵ Do you not remember that when I was still with you I told you this? ⁶ And you know what is restraining him now so that he may be revealed in his time.

---

opponent, one who **opposes** (other passages having the word are Luke 13:17; 21:15; 1 Cor. 16:9; Gal. 5:17; Phil. 1:28; 1 Tim. 1:10; 5:14). Second, he **exalts himself against every** object which mankind has chosen to worship (cf. Dan. 11:36). He will give place to no object of worship other than himself; he will tolerate no rivals in man's veneration.

With the expression, **so that,** the writers proceed to describe the result of the actions mentioned in the first part of the verse. The man of lawlessness reaches the climax to his arrogant assumptions in his claim to deity. Since **he takes his seat in the temple of God,** it seems impossible to regard **temple** as a reference to heaven itself for surely he would not succeed in such. Nor does it seem likely that he actually is in the church which is sometimes spoken of as the temple of God. It seems more satisfactory to regard the expression as meaning that he intrudes himself into the place or position which rightfully belongs to God alone. He occupies the position only in a manner of usurpation and not in fact or by right (cf. Ezek. 28:2).

[5] Though the plural is used in much of the epistle, Paul now uses the singular as he reminds the Thessalonians of his teaching when he was among them. **I told you** is in the imperfect tense in the Greek indicating that he had told them more than once. "I was telling you" would be an exact translation. It seems that Paul had told the Thessalonians all of **this** in more exact detail than he writes of it and that they were thus in a better position to understand the precise meaning of what he writes than is a modern interpreter.

[6] Paul alludes to something else the Thessalonians **know.** He had evidently spoken more plainly of this when

⁷ For the mystery of lawlessness is already at work; only he
who now restrains it will do so until he is out of the way.

---

he was in Thessalonica and feels that a reminder is all that
is now needed. If the modern reader were acquainted with
all that the Thessalonians knew, he would be able to understand the passage better. Doubtless, the writers had good
reason for writing in an apocalyptic style. It may well be
that they felt this lesson to be a special need for a limited
and local situation and so did not elaborate in such a way
that it would be understood by future readers as clearly as
by the Thessalonians. At any rate, there was something,
some person or power that was preventing the man of
lawlessness from being revealed at that time. The purpose
of the restraining power was that the man of lawlessness
may be revealed in his time. His revelation is an event to be
permitted by God but it will be at the time when God
wishes it to be.

[7] The word **mystery** is often used in the New Testament to indicate some aspect of the gospel which had been
kept secret and which human ingenuity could not discover
(e.g., Rom. 16:25; Eph. 1:9; 3:3, 4; 6:19; Col. 1:26, 27). The
thought is often added that the mystery has been revealed.
Paul knew that the spirit **of lawlessness** was **already at
work** but that there would be a certain mystery about it
until the revelation of the man of lawlessness. **He who now
restrains,** say the writers, is preventing the full manifestation. This, too, is a mystery which has not fully been revealed. However, Paul contemplates a time when the restrainer will be **out of the way;** he does not explain how this
removal will be brought about. It is noticeable that he
refers to the one **who restrains** as **he who,** while in verse 6
he employs the neuter **what.** Thus Paul seems to regard the
restrainer as both personal and impersonal. Evidently, there
is a sense in which the one restraining can be viewed in
either way. It may be that in one instance Paul regards the
restrainer as a power and in the other as a person.

⁸ And then the lawless one will be revealed, and the Lord
Jesus will slay him with the breath of his mouth and
destroy him by his appearing and his coming. ⁹ The coming of the lawless one by the activity of Satan will be with
all power and with pretended signs and wonders,

---

[8] As the writers pen these words, lawlessness is working in secret, in mystery; there will come a time when it
will have free course to show itself. It will be revealed in
the lawless one, the same being referred to previously as
"the man of lawlessness" and "the son of perdition." The
writers give no indication of how long it would be until the
revelation of this one. Likely they did not know. Inspiration
did not give omniscience. They are concerned about, not a
chronological timetable, but preventing the Thessalonians
from being alarmed and excited over thinking that the day
of the Lord has come. They want them to remember that
the rebellion and the revelation of the man of lawlessness
will precede that event.

With a relative clause Paul describes the fate of the man
of lawlessness at the coming of Christ. The Greek literally
has "whom the Lord Jesus will slay with the breath of his
mouth and destroy by the brightness of his coming." The
idea of slaying with his breath seems to indicate the ease
with which the Lord will defeat this foe (cf. Isa. 11:4; Rev.
19:15). The very radiance of his coming will devastate this
one whose ultimate doom is eternal perdition. Again, it
should be noted that the writers do not indicate how long it
will be after the manifestation of the man of sin before
Jesus comes and brings him to nought. This is another thing
they likely did not know, another facet of the subject which
must be classed in the realm of "mystery."

[9] The writers, speaking of the coming of the lawless
one, use the word *parousia*, a word characteristically used
to refer to the coming of Jesus (see notes on 1 Thess. 2:19).
The lawless one will have his *parousia* even as the Lord
will have his *parousia*. And he will come with power.

155

¹⁰ and with all wicked deception for those who are to
perish, because they refused to love the truth and so be
saved.

However, his power comes from **Satan;** his working will be
a manifestation of satanic activity (cf. Matt. 24:24). **Signs
and wonders,** words used of the miracles of the Lord and
the apostles (e.g., Acts 2:22, 43; 4:30; Heb. 2:4), are also
used of the work of the **lawless one.** However, his will be
counterfeit or **pretended.** The writers show the similarity
between this one and Jesus and yet they show the striking
contrast. Both are energized by a supernatural force; both
work signs and wonders; both will have a *parousia.* But the
supernatural force behind the lawless one is satanic; the
signs and wonders are pretended. And his *parousia* will so
far be eclipsed by the *parousia* of Jesus that the mere
breath of the Lord and the splendor of his presence will
defeat the lawless one.

[10] Having described the lawless one, the writers now
turn to a discussion of his effect upon men. He will come
with all wicked deception for those who are to perish.
Within the realm of his circumscribed activity his power
will be great. **All wicked deception** will be at his disposal.
This indicates every type of deception which wickedness
might devise. He knows he is a deceiver and intends to
deceive. His deception is intended **for those who are to
perish.** The present participle is used in the Greek construction and literally means "those who are perishing." Thus the
deception which wickedness devises is aimed primarily at
those who are already in a perishing condition. Why does
he wish to deceive those who are already perishing? He
wants them to remain in a perishing condition, to go on
perishing. Also, he wants to bring them down to a greater
depth of sin. And, evidently, he is not content that they
remain passively in a perishing condition; he wants to enlist
them in his active and militant rebellion. But why are these
in a perishing condition? **Because they refused to love the**

¹¹ Therefore God sends upon them a strong delusion, to make them believe what is false,

---

truth and so be saved. This indicates that they have heard the gospel. But they **refused to love the truth;** by a deliberate refusal on their part they did not welcome it (see notes on 1 Thess. 2:13; cf. Rom. 2:8). The words **and so be saved** are, in the Greek, a clause expressing purpose. Some loved the truth with a view to their salvation. These did not receive a love of the truth in order that they might be saved.

[11] The word **therefore** of verse 11 looks back to the statement of verse 10 concerning those perishing. They refused to love the truth. Therefore, "because they refused to love the truth and so be saved," **God sends upon them a strong delusion.** In what sense does God send delusions? The Old Testament says that God hardened Pharaoh's heart (Ex. 9:12); yet it is said that Pharaoh hardened his own heart (Ex. 8:32). God hardened Pharaoh's heart through the very means that were intended to work the opposite result. Pharaoh hardened his own heart by reacting to God's plea in the very opposite manner from that which God intended. Also, an action of David is said to be incited by Satan (1 Chron. 21:1); yet the action is ascribed to God (2 Sam. 24:1). How can an act of Satan be called also an act of God? In the sense that God permits Satan to perform the act and in the sense that the act is in harmony with the processes of a world with moral significance and order. Concerning a people who refused the knowledge of God and who preferred a lie to the truth, Paul repeatedly says that "God gave them up" (Rom. 1:24, 26, 28). There is a time in the progression of sin when God gives a man over to that which he prefers. The man prefers a lie. Satan is ready to deceive by means of lies. God gives the man over to the belief of the lie which he prefers. In a sense it might be said that the means by which a person is deceived is God's permissive agency—not God's direct agency. Satan

¹² so that all may be condemned who did not believe the truth but had pleasure in unrighteousness.

---

can go no farther than God permits. One way in which God's wrath is revealed is through the delusions, lies, suffering, corruption, dishonor, and the many other results of rebellion against God in which men find themselves after they harden themselves against the truth (cf. Rom. 1:18ff.).

The reason for God's permitting or sending the delusion is to make them believe what is false. The Greek more literally has "in order that they believe the lie." Since these did not love the truth, it is to be expected that they will love and believe the lie (cf. 2 Tim. 4:3, 4). God gives up people to a lie when they make it plain that they will not receive truth.

[12] The purpose of the sending of a delusion in order that men who do not love truth may believe a lie is stated: so that all may be condemned who did not believe the truth but had pleasure in unrighteousness. The sort of person who refuses to recognize and believe truth is the sort who will have pleasure in that which is the opposite of truth. He delights in sin; he obtains pleasure from unrighteousness. He will accordingly be judged, not merely as one who passively failed to embrace truth, but as one who refused to love the truth and who delighted in that which was the opposite of truth. As seen in Romans 1, his condemnation and misery are seen in the here and now but will especially be manifested in the day of the Lord.

Note on Apocalyptic Writings

Apocalyptic literature deals chiefly with the unseen or with the future. The Greek noun from which the word comes is *apokalupsis* and means "a revealing" or "an unveiling." It is the Greek word which stands as the title for the book of Revelation.

In the main, apocalyptic writings arose out of troublesome times. The Old Testament books of Daniel, Ezekiel, Isaiah, and Joel, all of which have much of the apocalyptic, were written after Israel had begun to suffer under the heel of foreign domination. A body of non-canonical apocalyptic literature, produced by the Jews from 210 B.C. to A.D. 200, is composed of a number of pseudonymous books among which are the *Book of Enoch*, the *Book of the Secrets of Enoch*, the *Apocalypse of Baruch*, and others. These reflect an unfavorable political background and despondency over the present. Some of the intertestamental books reflect the perilous days of the Syrian persecution led by Antiochus Epiphanes; later works reflect the iron hand of Rome. (See Vol. I, pp. 44ff., 53ff., 172f.) The only New Testament apocalyptic book, Revelation, was written during the persecution by Domitian. There are apocalyptic passages in other New Testament books. These, too, were connected with dark days. The apocalyptic discourse of Jesus (Matt. 24:1-34 and parallels) had to do with Roman oppression of the Jews; the apocalyptic portion of 2 Thessalonians was written to a church that had felt bitter persecution from its beginning right up to the time of writing.

It is impossible to compile a list of characteristics which will apply to every apocalyptic work. However, there are some which generally apply. A "vision" is often the context, though this is not true with Jesus and Paul. The predictive element is characteristic, in fact, is the main thing. The prediction usually involves a wider grasp of the world at large than prediction of other types. The apocalyptist seeks to go beneath the surface in his predictions, to delve into the deeper mysteries and to find the underlying significance of that which is apparent to the sight. Apocalyptic is characterized by symbols. These symbols represent ideas with which those inside the movement were evidently familiar and those outside were not. There is also a dramatic element. "The Lord Jesus will slay him with the breath of his mouth" is highly dramatic (2 Thess. 2:8). At times the details are exaggerated for effect. Some of them are used in a detailed description of the overall picture and are not to be pressed in seeking the meaning.

The main purpose of apocalyptic was to strengthen faith and to give courage and hope. Apostasy was very likely in times of trials. The writers of apocalypses stress the virtue of loyalty and picture in vivid terms the final overthrow of evil and the vindication of God's cause. The present is pictured as a time of great suffering. In contrast, the future is pictured as a glorious day, a time of deliverance and triumph for the people of God and of complete defeat for their adversaries. Evil is presented under various symbols; the increase of evil is portrayed under various figures; and the final victory of God over his foes is likewise presented in a variety of ways (cf. Dan. 7:1-22; 8:19-25; 11:32-12:3; Matt. 24:5-31; 2 Thess. 2:1-12; Rev. 16:1-21; 19:11-21).

NOTE ON THE MAN OF LAWLESSNESS

The passage regarding the rebellion, the man of lawlessness, and the restraining one is one of the most difficult in the New Testament. Some features within it are clear but others remain enigmatic. The purpose of the writers is clear. They wish to comfort and strengthen the Thessalonians in the midst of persecutions by assuring them of the final victory of the cause of God and the ultimate defeat of those who oppose this cause. They wish to correct the state of unrest and anxiety which evidently existed among some and to prevent its growth and spread by convincing the Thessalonians that the day of the Lord has not arrived. Paul, in the midst of the discussion, reminds them of his teaching regarding these great events while he was personally among them. Either he had spoken more plainly while in their presence or had acquainted them with the imagery which he here employs. It is evident, therefore, that the passage yielded itself more readily to the understanding of the Thessalonians than it does to a modern reader. It may thus be that the writers intentionally designed the passage for a limited and local need. However, the modern student should examine the passage carefully and understand it as best he can. In the interpretations of the passage various identifications of the man of lawlessness have been made. The identifications most commonly found in works on the subject are the following:

(1) Some have identified the man of lawlessness with a certain Roman emperor, as Nero, or some other persecuting emperor, or to a line of Roman emperors. They would identify the restraining one as a certain predecessor or predecessors among the emperors. When that one was taken out of the way, the man of lawlessness would appear. A strong point about this position is that it provides an explanation of why Paul wrote in symbolic language; explicit references to the empire or to certain emperors would invite additional persecution if the letter should come under the observation of the officials. Another strong point is that certain later emperors did make the claim to deity and did demand worship. This position also offers a satisfactory answer as to why the restrainer may be referred to in an impersonal way in verse 6 and in a personal way in verse 7; the government could be thought of as an impersonal power or the restraining force could be viewed as embodied in a personal form in the emperor. However, a valid objection to the position is this: Paul contemplates the man of lawlessness being in existence and waging opposition at the time the Lord returns; the Roman empire has long ago ceased to be. In the light of this fact, how could the position be maintained that the fulfilment was connected with Rome?

(2) Others have identified the man of lawlessness with the papacy and the rebellion or apostasy with the hierarchical system of the Roman Church. They usually consider the restraining force to be the temporal power of the Roman Empire. They point to the fact that this apostasy arose from within the church (the temple), to the claims of authority

161

made by the papacy, to the claims of miracles, to the fact
that the system will apparently continue to the coming of
Christ. Those who oppose this interpretation do not think
that the claims of the papacy are as blatant and unlimited
as those predicated of the man of sin. They point to the fact
that the papacy claims infallibility only in certain areas,
and, further, that the idea of complete lawlessness does not
seem to comport with the operation of the system. There is
the possibility that the claims of the papacy will become
more pronounced with the result that they will more nearly
fit the description of the man of lawlessness; however, this
would be a matter of conjecture. The positive identification
of the man of sin with the papacy, and that exclusively,
does not satisfy many students of the New Testament.

(3) A view advanced by some of the more recent scholars is that Paul is referring to some type of speculation then
current which was borrowed from Babylonian or some
other type of mythology. They cite instances from Babylonian myths in which a great future conflict between the
forces of good and evil is contemplated. However, the
differences between these mythological conflicts and that
contemplated by Paul are far greater than a superficial and
passing reference would indicate. Not enough similarity
can be found to justify this position.

(4) Some scholars hold that the man of lawlessness is
the devil himself. He was working behind the scenes, so to
speak, in Paul's day. This is what is referred to as the
mystery of lawlessness, according to this view. Further,
Satan's work will become increasingly more effective and
eventually he will be clearly manifested for what he is and
will be destroyed at the coming of Christ. Some (not all)
who hold this view advance the idea that Satan will become incarnate and will martial his forces for a great rebellion. They usually regard the restraining power as the Holy
Spirit whose work will one day be restricted so as to give
Satan freedom to work without the Spirit's hindrance. In
favor of this view it may be said that much of Paul's

description of the man of lawlessness accords with what is known of Satan from other passages. His working was already evident in a number of ways in Paul's day. It would not be difficult to imagine his making the impious and blasphemous claims which Paul says the man of sin will make. That which keeps him in restraint may well be thought of as the Holy Spirit working through the gospel. Conceivably, there may come a time when the word will not have free course, when evangelism will be restricted or even prohibited. The destruction of Satan at the coming of Christ will surely occur (Rev. 20:10). A weighty objection often brought against this view is that Paul says the coming of the lawless one is "by the activity of Satan." If his coming is according to or by the operation of Satan, then it is difficult to think that Paul intends to identify him with Satan. In opposition to the view that the restrainer is the Holy Spirit, it is often urged that it is difficult to conceive of the Holy Spirit or of God being "out of the way."

(5) Others hold that the mystery of lawlessness which was at work in Paul's day was the principle of evil; that eventually this force would grow until there shall be a great apostasy or rebellion against God; that the restraining force was government or possibly the principle of law and order; and that eventually a great leader, a human being, a man, will arise and will make the pretentious claims predicted by Paul. This view (as do most, if not all, of the others) considers the man of sin to be the antichrist (see 1 John 2:18). He and his followers will be defeated by Christ at his coming.

There are views other than the aforementioned ones, and there are divergencies among those who hold to one of the particular views. Not all who hold one particular view will concur in the identity of the restrainer, etc.

In drawing conclusions dogmatism is not in order. Though the mystery of lawlessness was at work in Paul's day, the coming rebellion and the revelation of the man of lawlessness were still future at the time he wrote. Many of

¹³ But we are bound to give thanks to God always for you,
brethren beloved by the Lord, because God chose you from
the beginning ᵇ to be saved, through sanctification by the
Spirit ᶜ and belief in the truth.

ᵇ Other ancient authorities read *as the first converts*
ᶜ Or *of spirit*

---

the details must be considered a mystery which Paul did
not explain in the epistle.

As a general summary it might be said that Paul saw the
force of evil working in his day, causing great suffering for
the followers of Christ. The full manifestation was being
held in check, likely by the force of law and order. Law and
order are deterrents to lawlessness and lawlessness is the
chief characteristic of the rebellion and of the one who
heads it. The attitude of disregard for law and rebellion
against God has been embodied in numerous groups and in
numerous individuals. Each of these might be considered
an antichrist (cf. 1 John 2:18). However, Paul predicted a
day when there would be a supreme embodiment in one
who would rebel against God and demand worship for
himself, claiming that he is God. This lawless one may be a
movement, an institution, a system, or even an individual.
Whatever may be his exact identity, his doom is certain. In
view of the nature of apocalyptic writings in general it may
be that Paul did not intend for specific identifications to be
made; it may be that he used the "man of lawlessness" to
portray, in apocalyptic fashion, the great conflict between
good and evil and the final outcome of each. It seems that
the student of the scriptures is able to obtain the main
lessons from the passage, to see the principal thrust of it,
without being able to identify positively each detail contained in it. The "day of the Lord" had not come, because
these events which must precede had not occurred.

Thanksgiving and Admonition, 2:13–15

[13] On the expression, **we are bound to give thanks
. . .** , see notes on 1:3. The affectionate address **brethren is**

again used; **beloved by the Lord** literally means "having been loved by the Lord." Thus the writers express their affection for the Thessalonians and also assure them of the Lord's affection for them. Both ideas would be of comfort and assurance to the Thessalonians. The word for **beloved** is a perfect participle, indicating that they had been loved by God and are still objects of his love. The expression of affection, the thanksgiving, and that for which thanks is given—all are in marked contrast to the dismal picture of the man of lawlessness and the fate of those under his deception—that which was discussed in the preceding section.

Because God chose you from the beginning states the reason for the thanksgiving. The variant reading "firstfruits" instead of "from the beginning" has good textual support and is preferred by some scholars. The word is used to refer to a "first convert" (Rom. 16:5) and to "first converts" (1 Cor. 16:15). If this reading be adopted, the meaning is that God had chosen the Thessalonians to be firstfruits of Macedonia, meaning first converts. Since their conversion occurred only a few weeks after that of the Philippians, they could, along with the Philippians, be called the first converts of Macedonia. However, **from the beginning** seems to have better textual support and is preferable. Some take this to mean from the beginning of Paul's ministry in Thessalonica. However, it seems best to regard the expression as referring to the original purpose of God (cf. 1 Cor. 2:7; Eph. 1:4; 3:5, 6, 11). It was in God's purpose to call Gentiles as well as Jews into his kingdom. He planned the redemptive work of Christ and the subsequent establishment of the kingdom long before these events transpired. In his purpose he chose a people for his own possession. He planned the ways and means by which this would be effected. This does not mean that he chose certain individuals unconditionally. The choice of God becoming effectual in any given case would be dependent upon that person's hearing the call and responding to it (vs. 14). **To be saved**

¹⁴ To this he called you through our gospel, so that you may
obtain the glory of our Lord Jesus Christ.

---

states the purpose God had in view in the divine choice (cf.
1 Thess. 4:7; 5:9).

The means through which salvation is effected is
through sanctification by the Spirit and belief in the truth.
Jesus once prayed: "Sanctify them in the truth; thy word is
truth" (John 17:17). Paul states that "the sword of the Spirit
. . . is the word of God" (Eph. 6:17). Since the word of
truth is the instrument or sword of the Spirit, it can readily
be seen that there is a close connection between the work
of the Spirit and the word of God. The Spirit accomplishes
sanctification through the word. A person is sanctified at
the time of conversion. Thus Paul could speak of the Cor-
inthian Christians as "those sanctified" (1 Cor. 1:2). However, there is a sense in which a child of God is being
sanctified and saved (see notes on 1 Thess. 4:3). In addition to being a past act and a present process, both salvation and sanctification may be viewed as a future goal. In
his first letter to the Thessalonians Paul expressed a prayer
that God would sanctify them wholly (see notes on 1
Thess. 5:23). Elsewhere Paul declared that "salvation is
nearer to us now than when we first believed" (Rom.
13:11). It seems likely that this ultimate goal of salvation
and sanctification is before the minds of the writers in the
present verse. Christians are constantly being set apart,
sanctified, made more holy, by the Holy Spirit as he works
through the truth. Again, the strong contrast between this
passage and that of the previous verses is noted. In the
previous section the writers had spoken somewhat at length
of deceit and of belief of a lie. Now a different note is struck
as they speak affectionately to a people whom God has
chosen for salvation—a salvation wrought through sanctification by the Spirit and belief of the truth (cf. vs. 12).

[14] God had called the Thessalonians to this, referring
to the salvation mentioned in verse 13. Called refers to a

¹⁵ So then, brethren, stand firm and hold to the traditions
which you were taught by us, either by word of mouth or
by letter.

---

past act, namely the preaching of the gospel and the ac-
cepting of it by the Thessalonians (see Acts 17:1-4). God's
call is prominent in these letters (1 Thess. 2:12; 4:7; 5:24).
The writers make clear how God had called these people:
through our gospel. The gospel is God's message of calling;
the preaching of the gospel is the medium through which
this call comes to man; the reception of the gospel is the
way in which this call becomes effectual.

Further, the writers assure the readers that God had
called them with a purpose in view: **so that you may obtain
the glory of our Lord Jesus Christ.** This looks forward to
the day of Christ's coming at which time his people will
share his glory, though there is a sense in which they share
it in this life (see notes on 1:12).

[15] The words **so then** show the logical connection
between the exhortation which follows and the statement
the writers have just made. Employing the affectionate
brethren, Paul exhorts the Thessalonians to **stand firm.** The
verb is a present imperative and urges them to continue to
stand firm. One of the main reasons for the writing of this
letter was that they might not be shaken (2:2; regarding
standing fast see notes on 1 Thess. 3:8 and also see Eph.
6:13, 14; Gal. 5:1).

The writers also admonish: **hold to the traditions which
you were taught by us.** The verb translated **hold to** is
translated "observing" in Mark 7:3 and "observe" in Mark
7:4. Though the word **traditions** is sometimes used in the
New Testament to indicate something other than the gospel
(e.g., Matt. 15:3, 6; Gal. 1:14; Col. 2:8), it is used in a
favorable sense here (see also 1 Cor. 11:2; 2 Thess. 3:6).
The literal meaning of the word from which tradition
comes (*paradosis*) is "a giving over, giving up." Thayer
says it denotes "a giving over which is done by word of

[16] Now may our Lord Jesus Christ himself, and God our Father, who loved us and gave us eternal comfort and good hope through grace,

---

mouth or in writing," and that, objectively, it denotes "what is delivered, the substance of the teaching." In the present admonition Paul is urging the Thessalonians to hold fast to those truths which inspired teachers had given to them. These truths had been delivered **by mouth** when the writers were in Thessalonica; they have since been delivered **by letter,** the letter having reference to 1 Thessalonians. The Thessalonians are to hold fast to these truths. They are not to be shaken by anyone pretending a recent revelation, or by any report purporting to come from Paul, or in any other way (see notes on 2:2).

Prayer for the Thessalonians, 2:16, 17

[16] Paul does not expect the readers to accomplish everything concerning which he has exhorted them in human strength alone. In a prayer of few words he turns their attention to the true source of strength. The deep concern of Paul is seen in such prayers (see 1 Thess. 3:11-13 for a prayer which is parallel in structure but different in content). He prays that **Christ** and the **Father** may provide the needs of the readers. On the close relationship assigned by Paul to the Father and the Son, see notes on 1 Thessalonians 1:1. The mention of Christ first does not indicate precedence (cf. Gal. 1:1; 2 Cor. 13:14 for the same order), but the mention of both as being the common source of spiritual blessings does indicate a recognition of equality. The writers include themselves with the readers as being recipients of divine love. **Who loved us** may be considered as having reference to all that God has done for them out of his love for them. Further, **God gave us eternal comfort.** The comfort which comes from God is of an eternal nature in contrast with any sort of hope of a transitory nature which this earth may have to offer (cf. 2 Cor.

¹⁷ **comfort your hearts and establish them in every good
work and word.**

1:3-7). God also gave **good hope.** This hope is "our blessed
hope, the appearing of the glory of our great God and
Savior Jesus Christ" (Titus 2:13). The gifts of **eternal comfort** and **good hope** are to be viewed as issuing from and a
manifestation of the great love of God. Both gifts are thus
unmerited on the part of man; they are **through grace,**
bestowed upon man through the unmerited favor of God.

[17] Both verbs, **comfort** and **establish,** are found in the
first epistle regarding the purpose for the sending of Timothy (3:2 where see notes). However, in that passage the
word which is here translated **comfort** is there translated
"exhort." The idea is that of encouraging and strengthening. Hence, Paul is praying that God will **comfort the
hearts** of the Thessalonians by giving to them the inner
strength which they need. **Establish** also has the idea of
strengthening—strengthening so as to make more firm and
steadfast. This being made strong, this strengthening, is to
be **in every good work and word.** It will be evident in all
that they do and say, in every activity of life.

EXHORTATION, CHAPTER 3

The final section of the epistle may be classed as exhortation. The divisions are not exact for there are some exhortations in the previous sections and parts of this chapter are
not exhortations. However, in the main, it is in the nature of
exhortation.

The writers ask that the readers pray in their behalf to
the end that the gospel may spread rapidly and prevail
even as it had done among the Thessalonians. A second
object for which they ask the readers to pray is that they,
the writers, may be delivered from evil men. The second
object is closely related to the first, for the success of the
gospel will depend, in part, on the freedom of the mission-

¹ Finally, brethren, pray for us, that the word of the Lord may speed on and triumph, as it did among you,

---

aries from hindrances of adversaries. The writers realize that there is a strong aversion, among many, to the gospel (3:1, 2).

In contrast to the lack of faith among many, the writers assure the readers of the faithfulness of the Lord; they promise the Thessalonians that he will furnish strength and leadership. They express confidence that the Thessalonians will continue to do what they ask them to do. They add a prayer that the Lord will direct the Thessalonians into a closer relationship with the love of God and into the steadfastness which Christ himself displayed (3:3-5).

Paul next turns to matters in the church which need attention. The problem of idleness perseveres. Paul admonishes the members of the church to avoid intimate association with those brethren who live in idleness. Paul and his helpers had set an example of working while they were in Thessalonica, and they had taught that one's right to eat depended upon that one's willingness to work. They exhort the idlers to work and earn their own living; they appeal to the church not to grow tired of well-doing. They exhort the church to discipline any who might refuse to obey the instructions of this letter (3:6-15).

The writers, in concluding, express a prayer for the readers. Paul again speaks in the first person singular and adds some words with his own hand. With a benediction, he closes in his characteristic way (3:16-18).

Exhortation to Pray for the Writers, 3:1, 2

[1] On the word **finally**, see notes on 1 Thessalonians 4:1. Having expressed a prayer in the preceding chapter, the writers now ask for prayer in their own behalf. They employ the present imperative indicating that they want the readers to continue praying. Paul often shows his need for the prayers of other Christians (cf. 1 Thess. 5:25; Rom.

² and that we may be delivered from wicked and evil men; for not all have faith.

15:30-32; 2 Cor. 1:11; Phil. 1:19; Col. 4:3; Phile. 22). In contrast with the general request for prayer in the first epistle, the writers make specific requests. First, they ask the readers to **pray for** them to the end that the gospel may travel speedily among men (cf. Ps. 147:15). They also ask them to pray that the gospel will **triumph** in the hearts of men. The Thessalonians are to pray that the word will do for men what God intended it to do and that, as a consequence, its power will be seen and praised by others. This seems to be the sense of "be glorified," which is the literal meaning of the Greek and which the RSV has translated by the word **triumph.** In the comparative clause, **as it did among you,** the writers acknowledge the success of the gospel in Thessalonica. They thus compliment the Thessalonians and preface, in a tactful way, the strong admonitions which are to follow.

[2] Paul specifies the second object for which the readers are to pray: the deliverance of the missionaries from adversaries. It seems most likely that Paul has persecuting Jews in mind. The narrative in Acts records their activities against him in Thessalonica (17:5), in Beroea (17:13), and in Corinth, from which place he is writing the epistle (18:12ff.). It is not likely that the events of Acts 18:12ff. had set in at the time 2 Thessalonians was written; it cannot, therefore, be certain that Paul's request reflects a situation at Corinth. It may be, however, that some opposition had begun at Corinth and that Paul makes the request remembering his experiences in other places. At this stage of his ministry, Paul regards the Jews as the most determined enemies of the gospel (see notes on 1 Thess. 2:14ff.). For a similar request for prayer see Romans 15:31. Paul explains why such men are as they are: **for not all have faith.** Paul uses the word **faith** to indicate that such men do not accept Christ. The definite article before **faith** leads some to think

171

³ But the Lord is faithful; he will strengthen you and guard
you from evil.ᵈ

ᵈ Or *the evil one*

---

the latter is meant. There is very little difference between
the two ideas. Either one makes it clear that the opposers
are outside the church.

Expression of Confidence, 3:3–5

[3] Over against the idea of the lack of faith among
men, the writers affirm the faithfulness of God. Paul often
points to the fact that God is faithful to encourage his
readers (cf. 1 Cor. 1:9; 10:13; 2 Cor. 1:18; 1 Thess. 5:24).
Nor is it unusual for him to contrast the faithlessness of
men with the faithfulness of God (cf. Rom. 3:3, 4; 2 Tim.
2:12, 13). Once again the concern of the writers for the
Thessalonians is seen: they do not say that they expect the
Lord's faithfulness to be seen in their own deliverance but
in what he will do for the readers. **He will strengthen** them.
This verb, meaning "to make firm," is the same verb used
concerning the purpose for sending Timothy (1 Thess. 3:2).
James uses the same verb in exhorting Christians to establish their own hearts (James 5:8). Paul is thus assuring his
readers that God will lend reenforcement to that which
Christians are to do for themselves and for one another. He
is assuring them that what he had prayed for in 2:17 will
come to pass. Further, the Lord **will guard you from evil.**
Concerning God's part in guarding or keeping the Christian, see notes on 1 Thessalonians 5:24. Since the neuter
and the masculine are the same form in the Greek, it is
impossible to determine whether Paul is saying "evil" or
"evil one." The sense is the same regardless of the view
adopted. However, most commentators prefer to think that
a personal "evil one" is more in keeping with the concepts
discussed in chapter 2. The devil is so designated in a
number of places (Matt. 13:19; Eph. 6:16; 1 John 2:13, 14;

⁴ And we have confidence in the Lord about you, that you are doing and will do the things which we command. ⁵ May the Lord direct your hearts to the love of God and to the steadfastness of Christ.

5:18). It is noteworthy that Paul closely associates the ideas of being strengthened and being guarded.

[4] Having expressed confidence in the Lord, the writers express confidence in the readers. The expression, **in the Lord,** indicates that their confidence is not in men as such but is grounded on the Lord. For the expression **in the Lord** designating the ground of Paul's expectations, note similar statements in Galatians 5:10 and Philippians 2:19, 24. The verb **command** indicates an authoritative order. The cognate noun, translated "instructions," is found in 1 Thessalonians 4:2. Paul's confidence that the Thessalonians **are doing** and **will** continue to **do** what he commands is based upon his certainty of their conversion (see notes on 1 Thess. 1:1ff.), his knowledge of their connection with the Lord, and upon the report of Timothy. Again, this tone of commendation may be seen as a tactful way of leading into the charges which are to follow.

[5] As noted above, Paul's confidence in the Thessalonians is grounded in the Lord. Now, having expressed that confidence, Paul appeals to the Lord in prayer. He knows that it is only as they rely upon the Lord that his confidence in them will prove to be justified. He and his co-workers had expressed a prayer in the first epistle that God would "direct" their way to the Thessalonians. They use the same verb, praying that **the Lord** will **direct** the **hearts** of the Thessalonians. **The love of God,** in Pauline usage, denotes God's love for man (cf. Rom. 5:5; 8:39; 2 Cor. 13:14). Thus the prayer is that the Lord will direct the hearts of the readers into a deeper realization of the love God has for them which will, in turn, produce a deeper love for God in their own hearts. **The steadfastness of Christ** has reference to the patience which Christ, while on earth, manifested in

⁶ Now we command you, brethren, in the name of our Lord
Jesus Christ, that you keep away from any brother who is
living in idleness and not in accord with the tradition that
you received from us. ⁷ For you yourselves know how you
ought to imitate us; we were not idle when we were with
you,

---

the midst of adversity. The prayer is to the effect that the
hearts of the Thessalonians will be directed into a greater
realization of this endurance which will quite naturally
produce within them a similar kind of endurance. These
two qualities, **love** and **steadfastness**, will be especially
needed by the readers as they proceed to carry out the
commands which follow.

Concerning Treatment of Disorderly Members, 3:6–15

[6] **Command** is the same authoritative word found in
verse 4. **Brethren** indicates that the writers are speaking as
brothers to brothers; yet they speak **in the name of** Christ
whose messengers they were (cf. 1 Thess. 2:4-6). In the
first epistle they appealed to the church to "admonish the
idle" (5:14); they had also exhorted the church "to work
with your hands" (4:11). But the problem of idleness has
persisted; there is a possibility that it has even grown
worse. It is possible that some who thought the day of the
Lord had already arrived had ceased working. Now, however, the church is commanded to take sterner measures
than in the first epistle. They are to **keep away from** such as
are described. This does not prohibit any contact whatever
for they are to continue to warn these (see vs. 15). But it is
a prohibition against fellowship and intimate association
(cf. Matt. 18:17; Rom. 16:17; 1 Cor. 5:11). The kind of
avoidance is that which would cause the offender to be
ashamed (see vs. 14). Regarding the meaning of **tradition,**
see notes on 2:15.

[7] The writers appeal to the knowledge of the readers;
they have done this a number of times in the two epistles (1

⁸ we did not eat any one's bread without paying, but with toil and labor we worked night and day, that we might not burden any of you. ⁹ It was not because we have not that right, but to give you in our conduct an example to imitate.

Thess. 1:5; 2:1, 2, 5, 9, 10, 11; 3:3; 4:2; 5:2; 2 Thess. 2:6). On the word imitate see notes on 1 Thessalonians 1:6 regarding "imitators." Concerning the manual work of the missionaries while in Thessalonica see notes on 1 Thessalonians 2:9. **We were not idle** is in striking contrast to **living in idleness** of verse 6.

[8] The expression "eat bread" was evidently a Semitism meaning to obtain a living (cf. Gen. 3:19; Amos 7:12; Mk. 3:20 where RSV translates the same Greek expression by the word "eat"; Lk. 14:1 where RSV translates "dine"). Paul does not mean that they had never accepted an invitation to a meal, but that they had not depended on others for a living. In the first epistle he had called attention to the industry of himself and his helpers while in Thessalonica. He had done so with a view to showing that they were not mercenary charlatans and that their motives had been pure (see 1 Thess. 2:9 where also see notes on the expressions "toil and labor" and "day and night"). Paul dignified manual labor both by teaching and by example (see Eph. 4:28; 1 Cor. 4:12). He now refers to his toil by way of example which the idlers are to imitate. The motive in their working, **that we might not burden any of you,** was a rebuke to those who were living at the expense of others.

[9] Paul's refusal to accept financial support from the Thessalonians was the waiving of a right (see Luke 10:7 for the teaching of Jesus on this). At times Paul accepted support from churches; in Thessalonica he received such from Philippi (Phil. 4:16). But when he felt that such practice would cause his motives to be questioned or would in any way impede the progress of the gospel, he refused to claim his right. He later followed this course in Corinth and

[10] For even when we were with you, we gave you this command: If any one will not work, let him not eat.

then at still a later time wrote to them in much the same way he wrote to the Thessalonians (see 1 Cor. 9:12-14; see the entire passage, 1 Cor. 9:3-18, for a lengthy discussion of Paul's foregoing the exercise of certain rights).

To the reason of verse 8, "that we might not burden any of you," Paul adds another reason for their working: **to give you in our conduct an example to imitate.** On "imitation" see notes on 1 Thessalonians 1:6; on **example** see notes on 1 Thessalonians 1:7. Evidently, Paul had known, while he was in Thessalonica, of the tendency to idleness among some of the people. He and his helpers wanted to show by **example** that a Christian should be a worker. The Thessalonians should see that the belief of Paul and his companions regarding the coming of Christ was not such that it caused them to **stop** working. Paul taught this both by word and by example.

[10] Here is another insight into the substance of the preaching done by the missionaries in Thessalonica. They had declared that those not willing to work should not be supported by others. The same strong appeal to work had been made in the first epistle (1 Thess. 4:11). The tenses Paul uses are interesting. **We gave you this command** is imperfect, indicating that they had repeatedly urged this practice. **Will not** is present tense, indicating an habitual and constant attitude. It is the one who is lazy, who is habitually unwilling to work, that is not to **eat** at the expense of others. The repeated admonition, even the authoritative command, of the preachers while in Thessalonica; the added force of their own personal example; the admonition in the first epistle; and now the enforced authoritative command plus the reminder of the previous example and teaching—all of this impresses upon the Thessalonians in a most forceful way the importance of working for a living.

¹¹ For we hear that some of you are living in idleness, mere busybodies, not doing any work. ¹² Now such persons we command and exhort in the Lord Jesus Christ to do their work in quietness and to earn their own living.

---

[11] The writers now reveal why they are giving so much emphasis to the subject of work. They are hearing (present tense) that some of the Thessalonians are living in idleness. Perhaps Timothy had reported this and it may be that others had brought similar reports. Paul had known the existence of the problem when he wrote the first epistle (cf. 1 Thess. 5:14). But the problem has persisted. There is the possibility that it had grown worse due to speculations concerning the second coming. Paul knows that he must deal with the problem in a more severe fashion. He describes the offenders positively as living in idleness and negatively as not doing any work. However, they are doing something as is indicated by the word busybodies. There seems to be a play on words in the Greek which, transposed into English, would be something like "working at nothing but working all around." They are busy at the task of creating disturbances and at the same time are living at the expense of those among whom they seek to create the disturbance (cf. 1 Tim. 5:13). If the assumption be true that they were promoters of the speculative ideas, then it may be that they were going about in an effort to spread these ideas. The idleness of these persons gave them time for their disruptive actions.

[12] The writers address those of the sort mentioned in the preceding verse. They use the same authoritative word found in verses 6 and 10, command, and add the word exhort, a word with an affectionate and brotherly tone. Paul has every intention of restoring these people; he has no desire to alienate them. He emphasizes that he commands and exhorts in the Lord, that is, by divine authority. The substance of the command and the exhortation is that the

---

¹³ Brethren, do not be weary in well-doing.

---

idlers and busybodies **do their work in quietness and to
earn their own living.** The Greek literally has "their own
bread." This is in contrast with the bread of others which
they have been eating. **In quietness** has reference to the
disposition of mind which is to accompany their work. The
writers are urging a calmness and tranquillity of heart (see
notes on 1 Thess. 4:11 regarding the expression, "live quietly").

[13] Paul turns from the idlers to address the faithful
who, evidently, constituted the main body of the church.
They should not permit the few to prevent their own perse-
verance in good works. The Greek construction is of such
nature as to indicate that Paul is asking them never to
become **weary in well-doing.** It does not indicate that they
had become weary and that Paul is urging them to cease
from such. Jesus used the word from which the expression,
be weary, comes and which the RSV translates "lose heart"
(Luke 18:1). The word is elsewhere used in the New
Testament only by Paul (cf. 2 Cor. 4:1, 16; Gal. 6:9; Rom.
7:21).

The word from which **well-doing** comes is a compound
word, found only here in the New Testament. However,
Paul uses the two parts of the word as separate words
in other passages to indicate the same general idea (2 Cor.
13:7; Gal. 6:9; Rom. 7:21). The Greek word *kalon,* used in
this compound, indicates that which is right in itself rather
than that which does good or confers certain benefits as
would be indicated by the Greek *agathos* as used in Luke
6:9, 1 Timothy 6:18, and other passages. Paul is urging the
Thessalonians to do that which is excellent, good, that
which accords with God's will, in every phase of life. They
are never to become weary in doing such. They are never to
let opposition from without or disorderly conduct on the
part of some of their members cause them to lose heart in
doing the honorable thing.

¹⁴ If any one refuses to obey what we say in this letter, note that man, and have nothing to do with him, that he may be ashamed.

---

[14] Paul uses the present tense, **refuses to obey**, viewing the matter from the standpoint of the time when the epistle is being read to the church. Some have thought that **this letter** to which Paul refers (Greek, *the letter*) indicates a letter which he anticipates the Thessalonians will write him; they have taken the command **note that man** as being connected with "the letter." Thus, they have Paul telling the Thessalonians to note such a man in a letter they will write to him. This is very unlikely. In view of the command of verses 6 and 10, it is most natural to consider **this letter** as the counterpart to the expression, **obey what we say**. By the expression **this letter** Paul has reference to the epistle he is writing to the Thessalonians. In the face of possible pseudonymous letters (2:2) Paul stresses his own letters as the basis for action (2:15; cf. 3:17). If at the time the letter is being read to the church any one is still refusing to obey what this letter enjoins, the stern measures specified are to be taken.

The writers had taught regarding these matters when they were in Thessalonica (3:10); doubtless, Timothy had repeated the instructions relative to the same thing (4:11, 12; 5:14); now the second epistle admonishes in most forceful terms (3:6-12). It is after all of this that the church is admonished to **note that man** (cf. Matt. 18:15-17). The word **note** is found only here in the New Testament. It means that the church is to take special notice of who these offenders are and mark them out for special treatment.

The word from which the RSV derives the expression, **have nothing to do with him**, is found only here and twice in 1 Corinthians (5:9, 11) where the RSV translates "associate." The word has within it the idea of mixing with or of intimately associating with. The procedure commanded by

¹⁵ **Do not look on him as an enemy, but warn him as a brother.**

Paul amounts to a withdrawal of fellowship. Intimate association with such members would imply approval of their manner of life and would encourage them to continue in it. Paul intends that the faithful members treat them in such a way as to show their disapproval of such conduct and to show that they do not regard them as faithful Christians. Insofar as those being disciplined are concerned, the purpose of such treatment is **that they may be ashamed.** The disciplinary acts are thus to be viewed as means whereby they may be brought to repentance. Paul hopes that the disapproval shown by faithful Christians will cause the disorderly ones to see their true state and will lead them to be **ashamed** of their conduct. In commanding disciplinary measures, Paul always has uppermost in mind the restoration of the offender (cf. 1 Cor. 5:5).

[15] The conduct of the disorderly ones is to be censured by the faithful Christians in no uncertain terms. Their conduct, the very opposite of what a Christian's conduct ought to be, places a barrier between the disorderly and the other members. Another barrier is to be placed by the refusal of the faithful to have intimate association with the offenders. Too, the conduct of the disorderly, however few they may be, causes outsiders to lose respect for the church (see 1 Thess. 4:11, 12). With all of this considered, it can be seen that certain members could easily develop a wrong attitude toward the offenders. Paul knows this and pleads with members of the church **not to look on him as an enemy, but warn him as a brother.** If discipline is effected in a harsh and censorious manner, it will not have the desired effects (cf. Gal. 6:1). The Greek word which the RSV translates **warn** is translated "admonish" in the first epistle (5:12, 14). Paul used the word when he said that he "did not cease night or day to admonish every one with tears" (Acts 20:31). The word in the New Testament is

¹⁶ Now may the Lord of peace himself give you peace at all
times and in all ways. The Lord be with you all.

---

distinctly Pauline, being found only in Paul's speech in Acts
and in his letters (cf. Rom. 15:14; Col. 3:16). It might
appropriately be called a "brotherly" word. Paul urges the
Thessalonians to remonstrate, warn, and plead in a true
spirit of love. This shows, as observed in the notes on verse
6, that Paul does not expect the faithful Christians to refuse
to have any sort of contact with the disorderly.

Conclusion, 3:16, 18

[16] The writers closed the two sections of the first
epistle with a prayer (3:11-13; 5:23). They closed the principal section of this epistle with a prayer (2:16, 17). Now
they close the final section and the epistle itself with a
prayer. Paul desires that the readers be at peace among
themselves and, above all, that they be at peace with God.
He realizes that the source of such peace is the Lord. This
is reminiscent of Christ's promise to his disciples (John
14:27). Paul elsewhere identifies Christ as "our peace" and
speaks of his work as that of "making peace" (Eph. 2:14,
15). He elsewhere makes reference to "the God of peace"
(e.g., Rom. 15:33; 16:20; Phil. 4:9; 1 Thess. 5:23). His
reference to the Lord of peace is another indication of the
closeness with which he associates the Father and the Son.
In this prayer the writers remind the Thessalonians that in
the midst of all their troubles it is the Lord himself to whom
they must look for peace. This inner tranquillity of heart for
which the writers pray is a serenity which they trust the
Thessalonians will have continually, at all times, and regardless of outward circumstances, in all ways. But Paul
and his friends not only pray for peace from the Lord; they
also pray for the presence of the Lord himself: The Lord be
with you all. The all of this prayer is very inclusive. The
writers do not want any of the members of the church to
feel that they are not included. One may contemplate the

¹⁷ I, Paul, write this greeting with my own hand. This is the mark in every letter of mine; it is the way I write. ¹⁸ The grace of our Lord Jesus Christ be with you all.

---

various stages of maturity and the various states of mind existing in the church at Thessalonica and he may think of this all as including all of them.

[17] It seems that the writing up to this point had been done by a scribe. Now Paul takes the pen in his own hand and writes the closing words. This is what he customarily did after dictating a letter (cf. 1 Cor. 16:21; Gal. 6:11; Col. 4:18; Phile. 19). Paul says that this is his mark in every letter of his. However, he does not call attention to it in every letter. Some have suggested that he does so here because of a spurious letter or letters purporting to come from Paul's hand (cf. 2:2). Paul recognizes his authority as an apostle and desires that his writings be accepted for what they were, the word of God.

[18] The prayer with which Paul closes the letter is the same as that with which he ended the first letter (5:28) except that here the word all is added. It may be that his use of the word is due to his desire that all the members of the church, even those whom he has felt compelled to reprimand, realize that they are included in this prayer. He had begun and closed the first epistle by reference to the grace of God (1:1; 5:28). So also he begins and closes the second epistle by reference to grace. It is entirely appropriate that Paul end the letter with reference to that which occupies such a prominent place in his teachings—the grace, the unmerited favor, of the Lord Jesus Christ.